chicken

HOMESTYLE

chicken

MURDOCH BOOKS

contents

Versatile chicken

Incredibly adaptable and very easy to cook, can there be a meat that's more popular than chicken? Utilised to great effect by practically every cuisine known to man, the humble 'chook' is the star of a vast repertoire of recipes. From the tandoor ovens of Northern India, the tagines of Morocco, the woks of China and the sauté pans of France to the charcoal grills of Portugal and Southeast Asia, chicken is cooked every which way and with a wide variety of ingredients. It can be stewed, baked, poached, steamed, grilled and stir-fried. It takes as well to currying, smoking, crumbing and being fashioned into meatballs as it does to roasting whole, being chopped and tossed through a creamy pasta sauce or baked in pieces in a crusty pie.

Its liver makes lush pâté, its wings make delicious party food and its bones are essential to one of the kitchen's most vital ingredients, chicken stock. Add to its versatility and utter deliciousness the fact that chicken is a healthy form of protein, it's little wonder we love it so much.

Conveniently, we can purchase chicken from the supermarket in a variety of forms—as a whole bird, a fine mince, divided into pieces still on the bone, or as boneless thigh or breast fillets, to name a few. Obliging butchers will even bone a whole chicken, if required. The various meaty parts of a chicken are equally well-suited to the majority of recipes. Chicken breast is particularly lean, containing far less fat than the thighs and legs. It can dry out and become stringy if over-cooked so care needs to be taken when cooking chicken breast, especially if the skin, which protects the delicate meat from fierce heat, has been removed.

Chicken is quite perishable; more so than red meats. When purchasing chicken, make sure it is absolutely fresh—the meat should be a shiny, clear pink with no darkened, shrivelled or sticky patches. Any fat should be consistently bright and creamy in colour. Store it in the refrigerator for two to three days only or wrap well and freeze for up to eight weeks.

Starters

Chicken liver pâté with pistachio nuts and prosciutto

PREPARATION TIME: 20 MINUTES + 3 HOURS REFRIGERATION | TOTAL COOKING TIME: 15 MINUTES | SERVES 10

6 very thin slices prosciutto

40 g butter

60 ml (2 fl oz/¼ cup) olive oil

80 g (2¾ oz) finely diced bacon

1 onion, finely chopped

2 garlic cloves, crushed

500 g (1 lb 2 oz) chicken livers

3 bay leaves

80 ml (2½ fl oz/⅓ cup) sherry or brandy

125 g (4½ oz) butter, extra, softened

50 g (1¾ oz/⅓ cup) pistachio nuts, toasted

NUTRITION PER SERVE
Protein 4 g; Fat 20 g; Carbohydrate 2 g; Dietary
Fibre 0.5 g; Cholesterol 48 mg; 938 kJ (224 Cal)

1 Line a 1.5 litre (52 fl oz/6 cups) loaf tin with foil. Then line with the prosciutto so that it hangs over the sides, making sure each slice overlaps. Heat the butter and oil in a heavy-based saucepan and cook the bacon, onion and garlic for 5–6 minutes, or until the onion is softened but not browned.

2 Trim the chicken livers of any fat and veins. Add them to the saucepan with the bay leaves. Increase the heat to hot and cook the liver for 3–4 minutes, or until the livers are brown on the outside, but still pink on the inside.

3 Add the sherry and simmer, stirring, for about 3 minutes, or until the liquid has almost disappeared. Remove the bay leaves. Process the mixture in a food processor until very fine. Gradually add the extra butter and blend until smooth. Season, then stir in the pistachio nuts.

4 Spoon the pâté mixture into the tin and fold the prosciutto over to enclose it. Refrigerate for at least 3–4 hours before serving. Cut into slices to serve.

NOTE: *The flavour, colour and texture of the pâté will improve after two days, and will also become easier to slice. Keep refrigerated for three to four days.*

Line the loaf tin with the prosciutto with each slice overlapping.

Add the sherry and simmer until most of the liquid has disappeared.

Stir the toasted pistachio nuts through the chicken liver mixture.

Potted chicken

PREPARATION TIME: 15 MINUTES + 2 HOURS REFRIGERATION | TOTAL COOKING TIME: 1 HOUR | SERVES 6

6 boneless, skinless chicken thighs
1 onion, sliced
1 carrot, sliced
6 peppercorns
1 bay leaf
pinch ground mace
pinch cayenne pepper
¼ teaspoon freshly grated nutmeg
200 g (7 oz) unsalted butter, softened

1   Place the chicken thighs, onion, carrot, peppercorns and bay leaf in a saucepan and add 500 ml (17 fl oz/2 cups) of water. Bring to the boil, skimming off any foam. Reduce the heat, then cover and simmer for 30 minutes, or until the chicken is tender and cooked through.

2   Remove the chicken, then rapidly boil the remaining liquid until it has reduced to about 60 ml (2 fl oz/¼ cup). Strain through a fine sieve and allow to cool.

3   Shred the chicken flesh and place in a food processor with the liquid and process until smooth. Add the mace, cayenne pepper, nutmeg and 150 g (5½ oz) of the butter. Season to taste with salt and freshly ground pepper and process until combined and smooth.

4   Put the chicken mixture in a 750 ml (26 fl oz/3 cup) ceramic dish. Melt the remaining butter in a small pan and pour the yellow clarified butter onto the surface of the chicken, leaving the white milk solids in the pan. Refrigerate for 2 hours, or until the butter sets.

NOTE: *To make clarified butter, gently melt the butter over low heat, skimming any foam off the top, without stirring. When the butter is melted, remove from the heat and leave to stand for 1 minute until the milk solids settle to the bottom. Carefully pour the yellow clarified butter over the dish, discard the solids in the pan.*

Strain the liquid through a fine sieve and leave to cool.

Carefully pour the yellow clarified butter over the potted chicken.

NUTRITION PER SERVE
Protein 25 g; Fat 30 g; Carbohydrate 1.5 g; Dietary Fibre 0.5 g; Cholesterol 140 mg; 1590 kJ (380 Cal)

Chicken and lemon meatballs

PREPARATION TIME: 20 MINUTES + 30 MINUTES REFRIGERATION | TOTAL COOKING TIME: 10 MINUTES | SERVES 4

500 g (1 lb 2 oz) minced (ground) chicken
2 garlic cloves, crushed
80 g (2¾ oz/1 cup) fresh white breadcrumbs
1 teaspoon grated lemon zest
1 teaspoon lemon thyme
1 egg, lightly beaten
1 tablespoon olive oil
2 tablespoons lemon juice

YOGHURT MINT SAUCE
200 g (7 oz) plain yoghurt
1 tablespoon shredded mint
rinsed, chopped zest from ¼ of a preserved
    lemon

1   Using your hands, mix the minced chicken, garlic, breadcrumbs, lemon zest, thyme, egg and some salt and freshly ground pepper together in a large bowl. Wet your hands and form tablespoons of the mixture into balls and place on a lined tray. Refrigerate for 30 minutes.

2   To make the yoghurt mint sauce, mix the yoghurt, mint and preserved lemon zest together.

3   Heat the oil in a non-stick frying pan and cook the chicken meatballs in two batches until golden on all sides and cooked through. Sprinkle with the lemon juice, transfer to a serving dish and sprinkle with more salt. Serve with the yoghurt mint sauce.

NUTRITION PER SERVE
Protein 35 g; Fat 11 g; Carbohydrate 16 g; Dietary
Fibre 1 g; Cholesterol 116 mg; 1300 kJ (310 Cal)

Combine the chicken, garlic, breadcrumbs, lemon zest, thyme, egg, salt and pepper.

Using wet hands, roll tablespoons of the mixture into balls.

Chicken quesadillas

PREPARATION TIME: 45 MINUTES + 1 HOUR MARINATING | TOTAL COOKING TIME: 20–30 MINUTES | SERVES 4

4 large green chillies
3 large red chillies
2 boneless, skinless chicken breasts
3 tablespoons wholegrain mustard
2 tablespoons honey
6 spring onions (scallions), thinly sliced
1–2 small red chillies, thinly sliced, optional
1–2 small green chillies, thinly sliced, optional
375 g (13 oz/3 cups) grated cheddar cheese
4 flour tortillas
olive oil, for cooking

GREEN CHILLI SALSA
3 long green chillies, thinly sliced
2 tomatoes, peeled, seeded and chopped
1 onion, finely chopped
4 tablespoons coriander (cilantro) leaves, finely chopped
2 tablespoons lime juice

NUTRITION PER SERVE
Protein 45 g; Fat 35 g; Carbohydrate 40 g; Dietary Fibre 5 g; Cholesterol 125 mg; 2665 kJ (635 Cal)

1 Place the large chillies under a hot grill (broiler) and cook for 5–8 minutes, turning frequently, until the skins are blackened. Allow to cool in a plastic bag. Remove the skin and seeds. Cut chillies in half, then slice into thin strips. Place the chicken in a shallow non-metallic dish. Combine the mustard and honey and add to the chicken. Turn the meat until well coated with the mixture. Cover and refrigerate for 1 hour. Place the chicken under a hot grill and cook for 4 minutes each side, or until cooked through and tender. Cool, then cut into thin strips.

2 To make the green chilli salsa, combine all the ingredients in a bowl and mix well, adding a little more lime juice if desired. Set aside.

3 Mix the chicken strips, spring onion, roasted chilli, sliced chilli and the cheddar together in a large bowl. Lightly grease a large, heavy-based frying pan and warm over medium heat. Place one tortilla in the pan and sprinkle with half of the chicken mix and top with another tortilla. Brush lightly with a little oil, invert the quesadilla onto a plate and then slide back into the pan so that the top becomes the bottom. Cook for a few minutes longer, just until the cheddar has melted and the underside looks golden and crisp. Slide the quesadilla onto a plate and keep warm.

4 Repeat with another tortilla and the remaining chicken mix. Top with the last tortilla. Cut into quarters and serve immediately, with the salsa.

Remove the blackened skins from the grilled, cooled chillies.

Turn the chicken to coat well with the mustard and honey mixture.

Cover the cheddar cheese, chicken, chilli and spring onion filling with another tortilla.

New potato, chicken and spinach frittata

PREPARATION TIME: 30 MINUTES | TOTAL COOKING TIME: 1 HOUR 15 MINUTES | SERVES 6

600 g (1 lb 5 oz) new potatoes, unpeeled,
    sliced about 1 cm (½ inch) thick
oil, for brushing
1 small barbecued chicken
500 g (1 lb 2 oz) English spinach leaves, stalks
    removed
125 g (4½ oz) feta cheese, crumbled
50 g (1¾ oz/½ cup) grated parmesan cheese
1 handful basil, chopped
10 eggs, lightly beaten
10 semi-dried (sun-blushed) tomato quarters

1 Preheat the oven to 180°C (350°F/Gas 4).
Put the potato in a greased ovenproof dish,
brush all over with a little oil and bake for
40 minutes, or until cooked. Turn the potato
once or twice during baking. Allow to cool.

2 Remove the skin from the chicken, pull the
flesh from the bones and roughly chop the meat.

3 Wash the spinach, put in a large saucepan,
cover and steam for 2 minutes to wilt slightly.
Drain and allow to cool, then squeeze out the
moisture and chop. Mix with the chicken and stir
in the feta, parmesan and basil. Season with salt
and freshly ground pepper, to taste.

4 Brush a 24 cm (9½ inch) diameter non-stick
or aluminum frying pan with oil. Arrange half
the potato slices over the base and spread half
the chicken mixture on top, then repeat the
layers. Season the beaten egg and pour over the
top. Arrange the tomato quarters on top. Cook
over low heat for 25 minutes, or until the centre
is almost cooked. Take care not to burn the base.
Heat the frittata under a preheated grill (broiler)
for 7 minutes, or until set. Cut the frittata into
wedges to serve.

Build up the layers of sliced potato and chicken filling in the frying pan.

Place the frittata under a preheated grill until it has set.

NUTRITION PER SERVE
Protein 40 g; Fat 25 g; Carbohydrate15 g; Dietary
Fibre 4 g; Cholesterol 375 mg; 2080 kJ (500 Cal)

Chicken and leek parcels

PREPARATION TIME: 40 MINUTES | TOTAL COOKING TIME: 45 MINUTES | SERVES 20

1 tablespoon oil, plus extra, for greasing
3 boneless, skinless chicken thighs
    (330 g/11½ oz)
30 g (1 oz) butter
2 leeks, thinly sliced
1 bacon slice, finely chopped
1 garlic clove, crushed
60 ml (2 fl oz/¼ cup) white wine
60 ml (2 fl oz/¼ cup) cream
2 teaspoons wholegrain mustard
25 g (1 oz/¼ cup) grated parmesan cheese
10 sheets filo pastry
80 g (2¾ oz) butter, extra, melted

1 Preheat oven to 180°C (350°F/Gas 4). Brush a baking tray with oil. Heat the oil in a heavy-based frying pan. Cook the chicken for 5 minutes on each side, or until browned and tender. Remove from the pan and drain on paper towels. Allow to cool, then chop the chicken finely.

2 Heat the butter in a large heavy-based saucepan. Add the leek, bacon and garlic, and cook for 3–4 minutes, or until the leek is soft and the bacon is crisp. Add the chicken, wine, cream and mustard. Cook, stirring constantly, for 4 minutes, or until thickened. Remove from the heat. Season to taste with salt and freshly ground pepper, and stir in the parmesan. Set aside to cool slightly.

3 Lay a sheet of filo pastry on a flat work surface and brush with melted butter. Top with another sheet of pastry and brush with butter. Cut the pastry lengthways into 4 strips. Place 1 tablespoon of the chicken mixture at the end of each strip. Fold the end diagonally over the filling, then continue folding to the end of the strip, forming a triangle. Repeat with the remaining pastry and filling. Place the triangles on a greased baking tray and brush with butter. Bake in batches for 25 minutes, or until browned and heated through.

NUTRITION PER SERVE
Protein 5.5 g; Fat 6.5 g; Carbohydrate 4 g; Dietary
Fibre 0 g; Cholesterol 25 mg; 430 kJ (100 Cal)

Add the chicken, wine, cream and mustard to the bacon mixture, and cook until thickened.

Place the chicken mixture at one end of the pastry and fold diagonally over the filling.

Pumpkin and pesto chicken in filo pastry

PREPARATION TIME: 30 MINUTES | TOTAL COOKING TIME: 50 MINUTES | SERVES 4

4 boneless, skinless chicken breasts
1 tablespoon oil
250 g (9 oz) pumpkin (winter squash)
500 g (1 lb 2 oz) English spinach
12 sheets filo pastry
100 g (3½ oz) butter, melted
25 g (1 oz/¼ cup) dry breadcrumbs
100 g (3½ oz) ricotta cheese
90 g (3¼ oz/⅓ cup) good-quality pesto
1 tablespoon pine nuts, chopped

1 Preheat the oven to 200°C (400°F/Gas 6). Season the chicken breast with salt and freshly ground pepper. Heat half the oil in a non-stick frying pan and fry the chicken until browned on both sides, then remove from the pan.

2 Cut the peeled pumpkin into 5 mm (¼ inch) slices. Heat the remaining oil in the same pan and fry the pumpkin until lightly browned on both sides. Allow to cool.

3 Put the spinach leaves into a bowl of boiling water and stir until just wilted. Drain well and pat dry with paper towels. Layer 3 sheets of filo pastry, brushing each with some of the melted butter, sprinkling between layers with some of the breadcrumbs.

4 Wrap each chicken breast in a quarter of the spinach and place one on a short side of the filo, leaving a 2 cm (¾ inch) gap. Top the chicken with a quarter of the pumpkin slices, then spread a quarter of the ricotta down the centre of the pumpkin. Top with a tablespoon of the pesto.

5 Fold the sides of the pastry over the filling, then roll the parcel up until it sits on the unsecured end. Repeat with the remaining ingredients. Place the parcels on a lightly greased baking tray, brush with any remaining butter and sprinkle with the pine nuts. Bake for 15 minutes, then cover loosely with foil and bake for a further 20 minutes, or until the pastry is golden brown.

NUTRITION PER SERVE
Protein 35 g; Fat 40 g; Carbohydrate 30 g; Dietary Fibre 2.5 g; Cholesterol 132 mg; 2635 kJ (630 Cal)

Remove the spinach from the bowl of boiling water and drain well.

Top the chicken breast with a quarter of the pumpkin slices.

Fold the sides of the pastry over the filling, then roll up until it sits on the unsecured end.

Stuffed chicken wings

PREPARATION TIME: 40 MINUTES | TOTAL COOKING TIME: 20 MINUTES | SERVES 6

6 large chicken wings

FILLING
3 tablespoons chopped water chestnuts
½ teaspoon finely chopped garlic
1 tablespoon finely chopped coriander
   (cilantro) leaves
1½ tablespoons fish sauce
1 spring onion (scallion), finely chopped
250 g (9 oz) minced (ground) pork
oil, for greasing

1   Pat the chicken dry with paper towels. To bone the chicken wings, use a small, sharp knife. Starting at the drumstick end, slip the knife down the side of the bone, all the way to the joint, taking care not to pierce the skin. Snap the bone free. Start on the next joint with the point of the knife, taking care not to pierce the elbow.

2   Once the first part of these two bones has been freed, the bones can be pulled out and cut at the knuckle to release. Reshape the wings.

3   To make the filling, combine the water chestnuts, garlic, coriander leaves, fish sauce, a teaspoon of freshly ground black pepper, spring onion and pork, mixing thoroughly. Using a teaspoon, stuff the wings evenly with the filling, taking care not to overfill or they will burst during cooking.

4   Place the chicken wings on a lightly oiled steamer, cover and steam over briskly boiling water for 10 minutes. Transfer the wings to a cold, lightly oiled grill (broiler) tray. Cook the chicken wings under medium heat for 5 minutes on each side or until brown and cooked through.

Slip the knife down the side of the bone, taking care not to pierce the skin.

Pull the bones out and cut at the knuckle to release, then reshape the wings.

NUTRITION PER CHICKEN WING
Protein 30 g; Fat 2.5 g; Carbohydrate 1.5 g; Dietary
Fibre 0.5 g; Cholesterol 62 mg; 610 kJ (145 Cal)

Thai chicken balls

PREPARATION TIME: 20 MINUTES | TOTAL COOKING TIME: 40 MINUTES | SERVES 6

1 kg (2 lb 4 oz) minced (ground) chicken
80 g (2¾ oz/1 cup) fresh breadcrumbs
4 spring onions (scallions), sliced
1 tablespoon ground coriander
3 large handfuls chopped coriander (cilantro)
    leaves
60 ml (2 fl oz/¼ cup) sweet chilli sauce
1–2 tablespoons lemon juice
oil, for frying

1 Preheat the oven to 200°C (400°F/Gas 6). Mix the chicken and the breadcrumbs in a large bowl.

2 Add the spring onion, ground and fresh coriander, chilli sauce and lemon juice, and mix well. Using damp hands, form the mixture into evenly shaped balls that are either small enough to eat with your fingers or large enough to use as burgers.

3 Heat the oil in a deep frying pan, and shallow-fry the chicken balls in batches over high heat until browned all over. Place the chicken balls on a baking tray and bake until cooked through. (The small chicken balls will take 5 minutes to cook and the larger ones will take 10–15 minutes.) This mixture also makes a delicious filling for sausage rolls.

NUTRITION PER SERVE
Protein 40 g; Fat 8 g; Carbohydrate 10 g; Dietary Fibre 1 g; Cholesterol 85 mg; 1160 kJ (275 Cal)

Mix the spring onion, coriander, chilli sauce and lemon juice into the chicken mixture.

With damp hands, form the mixture into evenly shaped balls.

Fry the chicken balls in oil until they are browned all over.

Chicken curry puffs

PREPARATION TIME: 1 HOUR 30 MINUTES + 30 MINUTES REFRIGERATION | TOTAL COOKING TIME: 35–45 MINUTES | MAKES ABOUT 36

2 tablespoons oil

400 g (14 oz) minced (ground) chicken

2 garlic cloves, crushed

1 onion, finely chopped

3 coriander roots, finely chopped

2 teaspoons ground turmeric

1½ teaspoons ground cumin

3 teaspoons ground coriander

1 small potato, peeled and very finely diced

1 tablespoon chopped coriander (cilantro) leaves and stems

3 teaspoons soft brown sugar

2 small red chillies, finely chopped

60 ml (2 fl oz/¼ cup) fish sauce

1 tablespoon lime juice

oil, extra, for deep-frying

chilli sauce or satay sauce, to serve

PASTRY

185 g (6½ oz/1½ cups) plain (all-purpose) flour

90 g (3¼ oz/½ cup) rice flour

½ teaspoon salt

60 g (2¼ oz) butter

125 ml (4 fl oz/½ cup) coconut milk

NUTRITION PER SERVE (6)
Protein 3.5 g; Fat 4 g; Carbohydrate 7 g; Dietary Fibre 0.5 g; Cholesterol 10 mg; 335 kJ (80 Cal)

1 Heat the oil in a medium wok or pan. Add the chicken and cook over high heat for 3 minutes, breaking up any lumps. Add the garlic, onion, coriander roots, turmeric, cumin, coriander and the potato to the wok. Stir-fry over medium heat for about 5 minutes, or until the chicken and potato are cooked through.

2 Add the fresh coriander, sugar, black pepper, chilli, fish sauce and lime juice. Stir until well combined and most of the liquid has evaporated, remove from the heat and let cool.

3 To make the pastry, sift the flours, salt and pepper into a bowl and rub in the butter until the mixture is fine and crumbly. Make a well in the centre, add the coconut milk and mix with a knife until the mixture forms a dough. Cover with plastic wrap and refrigerate for 30 minutes.

4 Divide the dough in half. Roll one half on a lightly floured work surface to 3 mm (⅛ inch) thick, then cut into circles with an 8 cm (3 inch) cutter. Place 2 teaspoons of the filling in the centre of each circle, brush the edges of the pastry lightly with water and fold over to enclose the filling; press the edges to seal. Repeat with the remaining, re-rolling the scraps until the dough and the filling are all used.

5 Heat the oil in a large wok or pan (it should be only half full). Deep-fry the puffs, in batches, until puffed and browned. Remove from oil with a wire mesh drainer; drain on paper towels. Serve with chilli or satay sauce.

Stir the ingredients in the wok until well combined and most of the liquid has evaporated.

Add the coconut milk and mix with a knife until the mixture forms a dough.

Fold the pastry over to enclose the filling and then press the edges to seal.

Yakitori

PREPARATION TIME: 20 MINUTES + SOAKING | TOTAL COOKING TIME: 10 MINUTES | MAKES 25 SKEWERS

1 kg (2 lb 4 oz) boneless, skinless chicken thighs
125 ml (4 fl oz/½ cup) sake (Japanese rice wine)
185 ml (6 fl oz/¾ cup) shoyu (Japanese soy sauce)
125 ml (4 fl oz/½ cup) mirin
2 tablespoons sugar
10 spring onions (scallions), diagonally cut into 2 cm (¾ inch) pieces

1 Soak 25 wooden skewers in water for about 20 minutes to prevent them from burning. Drain and set aside.

2 Cut the chicken thighs into bite-sized pieces. Combine the sake, shoyu, mirin and sugar in a small saucepan. Bring the mixture to the boil and then set aside.

3 Thread the chicken pieces onto the wooden skewers alternately with the spring onion pieces. Place the chicken skewers on a foil-lined tray and cook them under a preheated grill (broiler), turning and brushing frequently with the sauce, for 7–8 minutes, or until the chicken is cooked through. Serve immediately, garnished with a few spring onion pieces.

NOTE: *In Japan, Yakitori is usually served as a snack with beer. The addition of steamed rice and your favourite vegetables turns these delicious kebabs into a satisfying meal.*

Use a sharp knife to cut the chicken thighs into bite-sized pieces.

Thread the chicken pieces and spring onion alternately onto the skewers.

NUTRITION PER SKEWER
Protein 9.5 g; Fat 1 g; Carbohydrate 3 g; Dietary Fibre 0 g; Cholesterol 20 mg; 270 kJ (64 Cal)

Lemongrass chicken skewers

PREPARATION TIME: 20 MINUTES + OVERNIGHT MARINATING I TOTAL COOKING TIME: 15–20 MINUTES I SERVES 4

4 boneless, skinless chicken thighs
    (400 g/14 oz)
1½ tablespoons soft brown sugar
1½ tablespoons lime juice
2 teaspoons green curry paste
18 makrut (kaffir lime) leaves
2 stems lemongrass

MANGO SALSA
1 small mango, finely diced
1 teaspoon grated lime zest
2 teaspoons lime juice
1 teaspoon soft brown sugar
½ teaspoon fish sauce

1   Discard any excess fat from the chicken and cut in half lengthways. Combine the sugar, lime juice, curry paste and 2 of the finely shredded makrut leaves, in a bowl. Add the chicken and mix well. Cover and refrigerate for several hours or overnight.

2   To make the mango salsa, put all the ingredients in a bowl and stir gently to combine.

3   Trim the lemongrass to 20 cm (8 inches), leaving the root end intact. Cut each stem lengthways into four pieces. Cut a slit in each of the remaining lime leaves and thread one onto each piece of lemon grass. Cut two slits in each piece of chicken and thread onto the lemongrass, followed by another makrut leaf. Preheat a barbecue flat plate or a large frying pan on medium-high. Cook, turning occasionally, for 10 minutes or until golden and cooked through. Serve the skewers with the mango salsa.

Cut each trimmed lemongrass stem lengthways into four pieces.

Thread a lime leaf, then the chicken and another lime leaf onto the lemongrass.

NUTRITION PER SERVE
Protein 25 g; Fat 2.5 g; Carbohydrate 15 g; Dietary Fibre 1 g; Cholesterol 50 mg; 710 kJ (170 Cal)

Chicken and lime hummus tortillas

PREPARATION TIME: 45 MINUTES + 30 MINUTES REFRIGERATION I TOTAL COOKING TIME: 10–15 MINUTES I SERVES 4

500 g (1 lb 2 oz) minced (ground) chicken
1 red onion, finely chopped
3 garlic cloves, crushed
2 tablespoons chopped mint, plus extra,
    whole leaves to garnish
2 tablespoons chopped parsley
2 tablespoons lime juice
2 eggs, lightly beaten
160 g (5½ oz/2 cups) fresh white
    breadcrumbs
2 teaspoons chicken stock (bouillon) powder
150 g (5½ oz/1½ cups) dry breadcrumbs
oil, for shallow-frying
4 large flour tortillas
lettuce leaves, to serve
1 large ripe avocado, sliced

LIME HUMMUS
300 g (10½ oz) tinned chickpeas, drained
    and rinsed
2–3 tablespoons tahini
2 teaspoons sesame oil
2 garlic cloves, crushed
60 ml (2 fl oz/¼ cup) lime juice
1 tablespoon finely chopped mint
½ teaspoon sweet paprika

1   In a bowl, combine the chicken, onion, garlic, herbs, lime juice, half the egg, fresh breadcrumbs, stock powder and some freshly ground black pepper. Use your hands to mix thoroughly. Shape 2 tablespoons of the mixture at a time into round patties, dip in the remaining beaten egg, then toss in the dry breadcrumbs, pressing them on firmly.

2   Arrange the patties on a tray, cover and refrigerate for 30 minutes. Just before serving, shallow-fry the patties in moderately hot oil for 2–3 minutes each side, or until golden and cooked through. Drain on paper towels.

3   To make the lime hummus, process the chickpeas, tahini, sesame oil, garlic, lime juice and a little salt and freshly ground pepper in a food processor until the mixture is a smooth, thick paste. Stir in the mint and paprika.

4   To serve, toast the tortillas under a grill (broiler) or place in a dry pan until heated and lightly browned on both sides. Arrange the lettuce leaves, a few chicken patties and some sliced avocado on each and sprinkle with some mint leaves. Serve with the lime hummus.

NUTRITION PER SERVE
Protein 45 g; Fat 40 g; Carbohydrate 125 g; Dietary Fibre 15 g; Cholesterol 30 mg; 4705 kJ (1124 Cal)

Dip the patties in beaten egg and then coat with the dry breadcrumbs.

Shallow-fry the patties for 2–3 minutes each side, or until golden brown and cooked through.

Process the chickpeas, tahini, oil, garlic, lime juice and salt and pepper until smooth.

Spicy chicken pasties

PREPARATION TIME: 30 MINUTES I TOTAL COOKING TIME: 30 MINUTES I SERVES 20

2 tablespoons oil
1 small onion, finely chopped
1 garlic clove, crushed
½ teaspoon ground coriander
½ teaspoon ground cumin
¼ teaspoon ground turmeric
¼ teaspoon chilli powder
300 g (10½ oz) minced (ground) chicken
50 g (1¾ oz/⅓ cup) frozen peas
1 tablespoon finely chopped coriander
    (cilantro) leaves
5 sheets ready-rolled puff pastry
1 egg, lightly beaten

1 Preheat the oven to 180°C (350°F/Gas 4). Line a baking tray with foil. Heat the oil in a heavy-based frying pan. Add the onion and garlic and cook over medium heat for 2 minutes, or until the onion is soft. Add all the spices and cook, stirring, for 1 minute.

2 Add the chicken to the pan and cook, stirring occasionally, for 10 minutes, or until almost all the liquid has evaporated. Stir in the peas, coriander and salt, to taste. Remove from the heat and allow to cool.

3 Using a small plate or saucer as a guide, cut 10 cm (4 inch) circles from the pastry with a sharp knife. Place a level tablespoon of the mixture in the centre of each circle. Fold over and pleat the edge to seal. Place on the tray and brush with beaten egg. Bake for 15 minutes, or until golden.

HINT: *The uncooked pasties can be prepared several hours ahead. Store, covered, in the refrigerator. Cook just before serving.*

Stir the peas, coriander and salt into the chicken and spice mixture.

Fold the pastry over the filling, then pleat the edges to seal and brush with beaten egg.

NUTRITION PER SERVE
Protein 6 g; Fat 12 g; Carbohydrate 15 g; Dietary Fibre 1 g; Cholesterol 27 mg; 811 kJ (194 Cal)

Chicken curry bags

PREPARATION TIME: 30 MINUTES + 30 MINUTES STANDING | TOTAL COOKING TIME: 1 HOUR | MAKES 10

125 g (4½ oz/1 cup) plain (all-purpose) flour
1 egg
1 egg yolk
310 ml (10¾ fl oz/1¼ cups) milk
50 g (1¾ oz) butter, melted
butter, extra, for greasing

CHICKEN FILLING

60 g (2¼ oz) butter
1 red onion, chopped
1–2 teaspoons curry powder
2 tablespoons plain (all-purpose) flour
310 ml (10¾ fl oz/1¼ cups) milk
60 ml (2 fl oz/¼ cup) cream
1 large cooked boneless, skinless chicken
    breast, finely cubed
1 small handful chopped parsley
2 hard-boiled eggs, chopped

1   Whisk together the flour, egg, egg yolk and half the milk in a bowl. Add the remaining milk and 1 tablespoon melted butter and whisk until smooth. Cover and set aside for 30 minutes.

2   To make the chicken filling, melt the butter in a frying pan over medium heat, add the onion and cook until soft. Add the curry powder and flour and cook for 1 minute. Gradually add the milk, stirring, until smooth. Cook until the sauce has boiled and thickened. Remove from the heat, add the cream, chicken, parsley and egg.

3   Heat a crepe pan and brush with butter. Pour 60 ml (2 fl oz/¼ cup) batter into the pan, swirling the pan to cover the base. Pour the excess batter back into the jug, adding a little more milk if too thick. Cook for about 30 seconds, then turn over and cook until lightly brown. Preheat the oven to 180°C (350°F/Gas 4). Place 3 tablespoons of the chicken filling in the centre of each crepe, gather up into a bag. Tie with kitchen string. Grease a baking dish, brush each bag with butter and bake for 10 minutes, or until cooked through.

NUTRITION PER CURRY BAG
Protein 13 g; Fat 19 g; Carbohydrate 14 g; Dietary Fibre 1.6 g; Cholesterol 123 mg; 1159 kJ (277 Cal)

Use a spatula to turn the crepe over and cook the other side.

Place 3 tablespoons of the chicken filling in the centre of each crepe.

Chicken satay with peanut sauce

PREPARATION TIME: 40 MINUTES + 30 MINUTES MARINATING | TOTAL COOKING TIME: 15–20 MINUTES | SERVES 4

500 g (1 lb 2 oz) boneless, skinless chicken thighs, trimmed
1 onion, roughly chopped
2 lemongrass stems, white part only, thinly sliced
4 garlic cloves
2 red chillies, chopped
2 teaspoons ground coriander
1 teaspoon ground cumin
1 tablespoon soy sauce
60 ml (2 fl oz/¼ cup) oil
1 tablespoon soft brown sugar
Lebanese (short) cucumber slices, to serve
chopped roasted peanuts, to serve

PEANUT SAUCE
125 g (4½ oz/½ cup) crunchy peanut butter
250 ml (9 fl oz/1 cup) coconut milk
1–2 tablespoons sweet chilli sauce
1 tablespoon soy sauce
2 teaspoons lemon juice

1   Soak 20 wooden skewers in cold water for 20 minutes to prevent scorching. Cut the chicken into thick flattish strips. Thread a strip of chicken onto each skewer, flattening it on the skewer.

2   Process the onion, lemongrass, garlic, chilli, coriander, cumin, salt and soy sauce in a food processor, in short bursts, until smooth, adding a little oil to assist the processing. Spread the lemongrass mixture over the chicken, cover and refrigerate for 30 minutes.

3   To make the peanut sauce, put all the ingredients in a heavy-based saucepan with 125 ml (4 fl oz/½ cup) water. Stir over low heat until the mixture boils. Remove from the heat. The sauce will thicken on standing.

4   Heat a chargrill plate or barbecue flat plate until very hot and brush with the remaining oil. Cook the chicken in batches for 2–3 minutes on each side, sprinkling with a little oil and brown sugar (this will help produce a lovely flavour and colour). Serve garnished with the cucumber and peanuts. Serve the peanut sauce as a dipping sauce.

NUTRITION PER SERVE
Protein 40 g; Fat 45 g; Carbohydrate 14 g; Dietary Fibre 6 g; Cholesterol 60 mg; 2600 kJ (620 Cal)

Thread one chicken strip onto each skewer, flattening it out on the skewer.

Add a little bit of oil to the lemongrass mixture to assist the processing.

During cooking, sprinkle the chicken with oil and brown sugar.

San choy bau

PREPARATION TIME: 1 HOUR + 30 MINUTES SOAKING | TOTAL COOKING TIME: 10 MINUTES | SERVES 4

8 dried Chinese mushrooms
1 small iceberg lettuce, washed
500 g (1 lb 2 oz) minced (ground) chicken
1 tablespoon soy sauce
40 g (1½ oz/¼ cup) pine nuts
1 tablespoon oil
1 teaspoon garlic, finely chopped
4 spring onions (scallions), finely chopped
10 water chestnuts, chopped

SAUCE
3 teaspoons caster (superfine) sugar
1 tablespoon bean paste
3 teaspoons cornflour (cornstarch)
1 tablespoon oyster sauce
125 ml (4 fl oz/½ cup) chicken stock or water

1 Soak the mushrooms in hot water for 30 minutes. Drain, then squeeze to remove the excess liquid. Remove the stems and thinly slice the caps. Refrigerate the lettuce to crisp it.

2 Place the chicken in a bowl and stir in the soy sauce. Heat a wok, add the pine nuts and cook over medium heat until golden. Add the oil and garlic and cook gently until it is pale gold. Add the chicken mixture and cook over high heat, breaking up any lumps, for about 5 minutes, or until cooked through. Stir the mixture occasionally. Add the spring onion, mushrooms and water chestnuts, and cook for 1 minute.

3 To make the sauce, whisk all the ingredients together until the sugar and cornflour have dissolved. Make a well in the centre of the chicken mixture and add the sauce, stirring until it thickens and comes to the boil, sprinkle with the nuts.

4 Separate the lettuce leaves and place in individual serving bowls. Spoon the chicken mixture into the lettuce leaves. Serve immediately and eat with your hands.

Add the spring onion, mushrooms and water chestnuts to the chicken mixture.

Remove the core from the lettuce and separate the leaves.

NUTRITION PER SERVE
Protein 32 g; Fat 20 g; Carbohydrate 70 g; Dietary Fibre 2.5 g; Cholesterol 63 mg; 1360 kJ (325 Cal)

Chicken tikka

PREPARATION TIME: 30 MINUTES + OVERNIGHT MARINATING | TOTAL COOKING TIME: 16 MINUTES | MAKES 10 SKEWERS

¼ onion, chopped
2 garlic cloves, crushed
1 tablespoon grated fresh ginger
2 tablespoons lemon juice
1 teaspoon grated lemon zest
3 teaspoons ground coriander
3 teaspoons ground cumin
3 teaspoons garam masala
90 g (3¼ oz/⅓ cup) plain yoghurt
750 g (1 lb 10 oz) boneless, skinless chicken
    thighs, cut into cubes

1 Soak 10 wooden skewers in cold water for 20 minutes to prevent scorching.

2 In a food processor, finely chop the onion, garlic, ginger, lemon juice, zest, coriander, cumin and garam masala. Stir in the yoghurt and 1 teaspoon of salt.

3 Thread 4–5 chicken cubes onto each skewer and place in a large shallow non-metallic dish. Coat the skewers with the spice mixture. Marinate for several hours or overnight, covered, in the refrigerator.

4 Cook the skewers in batches on a medium-hot barbecue flat plate or chargrill pan, or under a hot grill (broiler), for 3–4 minutes on each side, or until golden brown and cooked through.

NUTRITION PER SERVE
Protein 15 g; Fat 4 g; Carbohydrate 1 g; Dietary
Fibre 0 g; Cholesterol 55 mg; 420 kJ (100 Cal)

Finely chop the onion, garlic, lemon juice, lemon zest and spices in a food processor.

Take the skewers and thread 4-5 pieces of chicken onto each one.

Cook the skewers for 3-4 minutes on each side, or until golden brown.

Salads

Italian-style chicken pasta salad

PREPARATION TIME: 30 MINUTES + 3 HOURS MARINATING | TOTAL COOKING TIME: 10 MINUTES | SERVES 6–8

3 boneless, skinless chicken breasts
60 ml (2 fl oz/¼ cup) lemon juice
1 garlic clove, crushed
100 g (3½ oz) thinly sliced prosciutto
1 Lebanese (short) cucumber
2 tablespoons seasoned pepper
2 tablespoons olive oil
135 g (4½ oz/1½ cups) penne pasta, cooked
80 g (2¾ oz/½ cup) thinly sliced sun-dried
    (sun-blushed) tomatoes
60 g (2¼ oz/½ cup) pitted black
    olives, halved
110 g (3¾ oz/½ cup) halved bottled
    artichoke hearts
parmesan cheese, shaved, to serve

CREAMY BASIL DRESSING
80 ml (2½ fl oz/⅓ cup) olive oil
1 tablespoon white wine vinegar
¼ teaspoon seasoned pepper
1 teaspoon dijon mustard
3 teaspoons cornflour (cornstarch)
170 ml (5½ fl oz/⅔ cup) cream

1 Remove the fat and sinew from the chicken. Flatten the chicken slightly with a mallet or rolling pin. Place the chicken in a non-metallic bowl with the combined lemon juice and garlic. Cover and refrigerate for at least 3 hours or overnight, turning occasionally.

2 Cut the prosciutto into strips. Halve the cucumber lengthways, then slice.

3 Drain the chicken and coat with the seasoned pepper. Heat the oil in a large heavy-based frying pan. Cook the chicken for 4 minutes on each side, or until lightly browned and cooked through. Remove from the heat and cool. Cut into pieces.

4 To make the dressing, combine the oil, vinegar, pepper and mustard in a saucepan. Blend the cornflour with 80 ml (2½ fl oz/ ⅓ cup) water until smooth, then add to the pan. Whisk over medium heat for 2 minutes, or until the sauce boils and thickens. Add the cream, and salt to taste. Stir until heated.

5 Combine the pasta, chicken, cucumber, prosciutto, tomato, olives and artichoke hearts in a large serving bowl. Pour in the dressing and toss gently to combine. Serve warm or cold, sprinkled with the parmesan.

NUTRITION PER SERVE (8)
Protein 22 g; Fat 28 g; Carbohydrate 38 g; Dietary Fibre 3.5 g; Cholesterol 64 mg; 2070 kJ (495 Cal)

Cut the cucumber in half lengthways, then cut it into slices.

Cook the chicken until lightly browned, then cool and cut into pieces.

Combine the pasta, chicken, cucumber, prosciutto, tomato, olives and artichoke hearts.

Smoked chicken caesar salad

PREPARATION TIME: 25 MINUTES | TOTAL COOKING TIME: 15 MINUTES | SERVES 4

GARLIC CROUTONS

1 thin baguette
45 g (1½ oz) unsalted butter
125 ml (4 fl oz/½ cup) olive oil
4 garlic cloves, crushed

1 cos (romaine) lettuce, tough outer
    leaves discarded
1 large smoked chicken (about 950 g/
    2 lb 20 oz), cut into bite-sized pieces
150 g (5½ oz) parmesan cheese, shaved

DRESSING

2 eggs
2 garlic cloves, crushed
2 tablespoons lemon juice
2 teaspoons dijon mustard
45 g (1½ oz) tinned anchovy fillets, drained
250 ml (9 fl oz/1 cup) olive oil

1 To make the garlic croutons, slice the
baguette diagonally into 1 cm (½ inch) thick
slices. Melt the butter and olive oil in a large
frying pan over moderate heat. Stir in the garlic.
Fry the bread, in batches, until golden. Remove
from the pan and drain on paper towels.

2 Separate the lettuce leaves, wash and dry
thoroughly. Tear the larger leaves into pieces and
refrigerate until well chilled.

3 To make the dressing, process the eggs,
garlic, lemon juice, mustard and anchovies. With
the motor running, gradually pour in the oil in a
thin stream and process until thick. Season
to taste.

4 Combine the lettuce leaves, chicken, half of
the croutons and half the parmesan in a bowl
and toss with dressing. Spoon the salad in serving
bowls and sprinkle with the remaining croutons
and parmesan.

Roughly chop the smoked chicken meat into bite-sized pieces.

Process the eggs, garlic, lemon juice, mustard and and anchovies.

NUTRITION PER SERVE
Protein 45 g; Fat 120 g; Carbohydrate 10 g; Dietary
Fibre 2 g; Cholesterol 235 mg; 5350 kJ (1275 Cal)

Warm chicken salad

PREPARATION TIME: 15 MINUTES | TOTAL COOKING TIME: 15 MINUTES | SERVES 4

2 teaspoons cumin seeds
1 tablespoon olive oil
1 red onion, thinly sliced
3 garlic cloves, finely chopped
2 teaspoons finely chopped red chilli
1½ teaspoons sweet paprika
3 boneless, skinless chicken breasts, cut into
   bite-sized pieces
2 tablespoons lemon juice
2 tablespoons chopped coriander (cilantro)
   leaves
200 g (7 oz) mixed salad leaves
2 Lebanese (short) cucumbers, thinly sliced
12 Kalamata olives
2 tablespoons extra virgin olive oil

1 Dry-fry the cumin seeds in a frying pan for
1–2 minutes, or until fragrant. Remove and set
aside. Heat the olive oil in the frying pan, add the
onion and cook over medium heat until soft.

2 Add the garlic, cumin seeds, chopped chilli
and paprika. Cook, stirring, for 1 minute. Add
the chicken and cook, stirring, for 5 minutes, or
until cooked through.

3 Remove from the heat and cool slightly. Stir
in the lemon juice and coriander, and season
to taste with salt. Arrange the salad leaves,
cucumber and olives on a serving platter, drizzle
with the extra virgin olive oil and place the
chicken mixture on top. Serve immediately.

Add the chopped chicken to the pan with the onion and spice mixture.

When the mixture has cooled slightly, stir in the lemon juice and coriander.

NUTRITION PER SERVE
Protein 35 g; Fat 20 g; Carbohydrate 10 g; Dietary
Fibre 5 g; Cholesterol 105 mg; 1520 kJ (365 Cal)

Chilli salt chicken salad

PREPARATION TIME: 35 MINUTES | TOTAL COOKING TIME: 20 MINUTES | SERVES 4

1 red capsicum (pepper), cut into
    matchsticks (see NOTE)
1 yellow capsicum (pepper), cut into
    matchsticks
4 spring onions (scallions), cut into
    matchsticks
1 large handful mint
1 large handful coriander (cilantro) leaves
3 boneless, skinless chicken breasts
60 g (2¼ oz/½ cup) plain (all-purpose) flour
1 tablespoon chilli powder
1 tablespoon onion powder
1 tablespoon garlic powder
1 tablespoon finely crushed sea salt
oil, for deep-frying

DRESSING
1 tablespoon sugar
2 tablespoons lemon juice
60 ml (2 fl oz/¼ cup) rice vinegar
60 ml (2 fl oz/¼ cup) peanut oil

1 Put the capsicum and spring onion strips in a bowl with the mint and coriander leaves.

2 To make the dressing, put all the ingredients in a bowl and whisk until combined.

3 Cut the chicken breasts into thin strips. Combine the flour, chilli powder, onion powder, garlic powder and salt in a plastic bag or shallow bowl. Add the chicken in batches and toss to coat in the flour mixture. Remove the chicken and shake off any excess flour.

4 Half fill a large heavy-based saucepan with the oil. When the oil is hot, add the chicken in batches and deep-fry until it is golden brown. Drain well on paper towels. Add the chicken to the bowl with the vegetables and herbs, drizzle with the dressing and toss gently to combine. Serve immediately.

NOTE: *Matchsticks, batons or julienne strips are even-sized strips of vegetables, the size and shape of matchsticks.*

NUTRITION PER SERVE
Protein 20 g; Fat 30 g; Carbohydrate 20 g; Dietary Fibre 2 g; Cholesterol 40 mg; 1720 kJ (410 Cal)

Cut the capsicum and spring onions into fine matchsticks.

Remove the fat from the chicken and cut the breasts into long, thin strips.

Add the chicken strips into the spiced flour mixture and toss well to coat.

Thai chicken salad

PREPARATION TIME: 20 MINUTES | TOTAL COOKING TIME: 5 MINUTES | SERVES 6

1 cos (romaine) lettuce
2 tablespoons oil
1.3 kg (3 lb 10 oz) minced (ground) chicken
1 small handfull coriander (cilantro) leaves,
   finely chopped
1 small handful mint, finely chopped
1 small red onion, sliced
3 spring onions (scallions), chopped
80 ml (2¾ fl oz/⅓ cup) lime juice
2 tablespoons soy sauce
2 tablespoons fish sauce
1 tablespoon sweet chilli sauce
2 garlic cloves, crushed
2 teaspoons soft brown sugar
1 tablespoon finely chopped lemongrass, white
   part only
40 g (1½ oz/¼ cup) roasted peanuts

1   Wash and dry the lettuce leaves thoroughly.
Arrange on a platter.

2   Heat the oil in a heavy-based frying pan. Add
the minced chicken and 80 ml (2½ fl oz/⅓ cup)
water. Cook over medium heat for 5 minutes,
or until the chicken is cooked and almost all the
liquid has evaporated. Break up any lumps as the
chicken cooks. Remove from the heat.

3   Transfer the chicken to a bowl. Stir in the
coriander, mint, onion and spring onion.

4   Combine the lime juice, soy sauce, fish
sauce, sweet chilli sauce, garlic, brown sugar
and lemongrass in a small bowl. Season with salt
and mix well. Stir into the chicken mixture. Just
before serving, stir in the peanuts. Serve on the
lettuce leaves.

Cut the onion into slices and finely chop the
coriander and mint.

Break up any lumps in the chicken with a fork as
the chicken cooks.

NUTRITION PER SERVE
Protein 33 g; Fat 14 g; Carbohydrate 5 g; Dietary
Fibre 2.5 g; Cholesterol 62 mg; 1175 kJ (280 Cal)

Vietnamese papaya and chicken salad

PREPARATION TIME: 30 MINUTES | TOTAL COOKING TIME: 10 MINUTES | SERVES 4

2 boneless, skinless chicken breasts
2 tablespoons fish sauce
1 tablespoon rice wine vinegar
1 tablespoon lime juice
2 teaspoons sugar
1 large green papaya
1 large handful Vietnamese mint
1 handful coriander (cilantro) leaves
2 red chillies, seeded and thinly sliced
2 tablespoons chopped roasted peanuts

1   Place the chicken in a frying pan with enough water to just cover. Simmer over gentle heat for 10 minutes, or until cooked. Don't let the water boil—it should just gently simmer, to poach the chicken. Remove the chicken and allow to cool completely. Thinly slice the chicken.

2   Mix together the fish sauce, vinegar, lime juice and sugar, set aside. Using a potato peeler, peel the papaya, and discard the seeds. Cut the papaya flesh into thin strips. Mix gently in a bowl with the Vietnamese mint, coriander and sliced chilli.

3   Arrange the papaya mixture on a serving plate and pile the sliced chicken on top. Scatter the peanuts over the top. Drizzle with the dressing, just before serving.

NOTE: *Green papaya is underripe papaya, used for tartness and texture.*

NUTRITION PER SERVE
Protein 22 g; Fat 6 g; Carbohydrate 6 g; Dietary Fibre 1.5 g; Cholesterol 44 mg; 712 kJ (170 Cal)

Gently simmer the chicken breasts until they are cooked through.

Using a very sharp knife, cut the peeled papaya into long, thin strips.

Chicken and watercress salad

PREPARATION TIME: 40 MINUTES | TOTAL COOKING TIME: 10–15 MINUTES | SERVES 4

3 boneless, skinless chicken breasts
1 Lebanese (short) cucumber
½ red capsicum (pepper)
150 g (5½ oz) watercress
1 small handful mint
2 tablespoons crisp-fried onion (see NOTE)

DRESSING
60 ml (2 fl oz/¼ cup) lime juice
2 tablespoons coconut milk
1 tablespoon fish sauce
1 tablespoon sweet chilli sauce

1   Line a bamboo steamer with baking paper and steam the chicken, covered, over a wok or pan of simmering water, for 10 minutes, or until the chicken is cooked through. Remove from the heat and set aside to cool. Thinly slice the cucumber and cut the slices in half. Slice the capsicum into thin strips.

2   While the chicken is cooling, pick over the watercress and separate the sprigs from the tough stems. Arrange the watercress and whole mint leaves on a serving plate. Using your fingers, tear the chicken into long, thin shreds. Gently toss the shredded chicken, cucumber and capsicum in a bowl. Arrange over the watercress bed.

3   To make the dressing, whisk all the ingredients until combined.

4   Plate the salad, sprinkle with the crisp-fried onion and drizzle the dressing over, just before serving.

NOTE: *Crisp-fried, or sometimes deep-fried, onions are available in packets or small jars from Asian supermarkets.*

NUTRITION PER SERVE
Protein 40 g; Fat 6 g; Carbohydrate 3 g; Dietary Fibre 2.5 g; Cholesterol 82 mg; 966 kJ (230 Cal)

Pick over the watercress to separate the sprigs from the tough stems.

When the chicken is cooked, tear it into shreds, using your fingers.

Chicken and citrus salad with curry dressing

PREPARATION TIME: 20 MINUTES | TOTAL COOKING TIME: 15 MINUTES | SERVES 4

4 boneless, skinless chicken breasts
1 tablespoon olive oil
2 oranges
1 lettuce
250 g (9 oz) watercress, picked over
1 medium handful chives

CURRY DRESSING
3 teaspoons curry powder
2 spring onions (scallions), thinly sliced
2 tablespoons olive oil
2 tablespoons sunflower oil
1 tablespoon balsamic vinegar
2 teaspoons soft brown sugar
1 teaspoon chopped green chilli

1 Trim the chicken breasts of any fat and sinew. Heat the oil in a frying pan and cook the chicken over medium heat for about 7 minutes on each side, or until browned and tender. Allow to cool, then cut across the grain into thick strips.

2 To make the curry dressing, dry-fry the curry powder in a frying pan for 1 minute, or until fragrant. Cool slightly, then place in a small bowl with the remaining ingredients and whisk to combine. Season to taste with salt and pepper. Set aside to allow the flavours to develop.

3 Peel the oranges, removing all the white pith. Cut into segments, between the membrane, and discard any pips.

4 Wash and dry the lettuce leaves and watercress and arrange on a large platter. Place the chicken pieces and orange segments on top. Whisk the dressing again, then drizzle it over the salad. Cut the chives into short lengths and scatter over the top.

Dry-fry the curry powder in a frying pan for 1 minute, or until fragrant.

Carefully cut the oranges into segments between the membrane.

NUTRITION PER SERVE
Protein 25 g; Fat 25 g; Carbohydrate 10 g; Dietary Fibre 2 g; Cholesterol 55 mg; 1590 kJ (380 Cal)

Tandoori chicken salad

PREPARATION TIME: 20 MINUTES + OVERNIGHT MARINATING | TOTAL COOKING TIME: 15 MINUTES | SERVES 4

4 boneless, skinless chicken breasts
2–3 tablespoons tandoori paste
200 g (7 oz) thick plain yoghurt
1 tablespoon lemon juice
1 handful coriander (cilantro) leaves
60 g (2¼ oz/½ cup) slivered almonds, toasted
snow pea (mangetout) sprouts, to serve

CUCUMBER AND YOGHURT DRESSING
1 Lebanese (short) cucumber, grated
200 g (7 oz) thick plain yoghurt
1 tablespoon chopped mint
2 teaspoons lemon juice

1 Cut the chicken breast into thick strips. Combine the tandoori paste, yoghurt and lemon juice in a large non-metallic bowl, add the chicken strips and toss to coat well. Refrigerate, covered, and leave to marinate overnight.

2 To make the dressing, put the grated cucumber in a medium bowl. Add the remaining ingredients and stir until well combined. Refrigerate until needed.

3 Heat a large non-stick frying pan, add the marinated chicken in batches and cook, turning frequently, until cooked through. Cool and place in a large bowl. Add the coriander leaves and toasted almonds, and toss until well combined. Serve on a bed of snow pea sprouts, with a dollop of dressing on top or served separately.

NOTE: *The quality of the tandoori paste used will determine the flavour and look of the chicken. There are many home-made varieties available from supermarkets and delicatessens.*

Combine the tandoori paste with the yoghurt and lemon juice.

Using a metal grater, coarsely grate the unpeeled Lebanese cucumber.

NUTRITION PER SERVE
Protein 35 g; Fat 15 g; Carbohydrate 7 g; Dietary Fibre 2 g; Cholesterol 70 mg; 1230 kJ (290 Cal)

Red curry chicken salad

PREPARATION TIME: 30 MINUTES + OVERNIGHT MARINATING | TOTAL COOKING TIME: 20 MINUTES | SERVES 4

500 g (1 lb 2 oz) boneless, skinless chicken thighs, cut into thin strips
2 teaspoons Thai red curry paste
1 teaspoon chopped red chilli
1 garlic clove, crushed
1 stem lemongrass, white part only, finely chopped
cooking oil spray
1 red onion, thinly sliced
2 tomatoes, cut into wedges
2 tablespoons chopped mint
4 tablespoons chopped coriander (cilantro) leaves
400 g (14 oz) mixed salad leaves
2 tablespoons roasted peanuts

DRESSING
1½ tablespoons soft brown sugar
2 tablespoons fish sauce
2 tablespoons lime juice
2 makrut (kaffir lime) leaves, shredded
2 teaspoons oil

1 Combine the chicken, curry paste, chilli, garlic and lemongrass in a bowl. Cover and refrigerate overnight.

2 Lightly spray a non-stick frying pan with oil and cook the chicken in batches over medium-high heat for about 5-7 minutes until cooked through and lightly browned; set aside. Add the onion to the pan and cook for 3 minutes, or until just soft. Return the chicken and any juices to the pan and add the tomato, mint and coriander, stirring until heated. Set aside until just warm.

3 To make the dressing, put all the ingredients in a bowl and mix until well combined. In a bowl, toss the chicken mixture with the salad leaves and dressing. Sprinkle with the roasted peanuts, to serve.

NUTRITION PER SERVE
Protein 25 g; Fat 10 g; Carbohydrate 15 g; Dietary Fibre 2.5 g; Cholesterol 50 mg; 1050 kJ (250 Cal)

If you find it easier, you can use your hands to mix the chicken and marinade.

Stir the tomatoes and herbs with the chicken, until heated through.

Vietnamese chicken and cabbage salad

PREPARATION TIME: 40 MINUTES | TOTAL COOKING TIME: 5 MINUTES | SERVES 4

4 boneless, skinless chicken breasts, cooked
125 g (4½ oz/1 cup) thinly sliced celery
2 carrots, cut into thin matchsticks
75 g (2½ oz/1 cup) finely shredded cabbage
1 small onion, sliced
1 small handful coriander (cilantro) leaves
4 tablespoons finely shredded mint

DRESSING
60 g (2¼ oz/¼ cup) caster (superfine) sugar
1 tablespoon fish sauce
1 teaspoon crushed garlic
2 tablespoons white vinegar
1 red chilli, seeded and finely chopped

TOPPING
2 tablespoons peanut oil
1½ teaspoons chopped garlic
50 g (1¾ oz/⅓ cup) roasted peanuts, finely
    chopped
1 tablespoon caster (superfine) sugar

1 Cut the cooked chicken breasts into long, thin strips. Combine the chicken, celery, carrot, cabbage, onion, coriander and mint in a bowl.

2 To make the dressing, put all the ingredients and 2 tablespoons water in a small bowl. Whisk until the sugar has dissolved and the ingredients are well combined. Pour the dressing over the chicken mixture and toss to combine. Arrange on a serving plate.

3 To make the topping, heat the oil in a wok over medium heat. Add the garlic and cook, stirring, until pale golden. Stir in the peanuts and sugar. Cool slightly. Sprinkle the topping over the salad just before serving.

Pour the dressing over the salad and gently toss to combine.

Gently stir the peanuts and sugar into the cooked garlic.

NUTRITION PER SERVE
Protein 50 g; Fat 15 g; Carbohydrate 25 g; Dietary Fibre 3 g; Cholesterol 110 mg; 1820 kJ (435 Cal)

Pacific chicken salad

PREPARATION TIME: 20 MINUTES | TOTAL COOKING TIME: 15 MINUTES | SERVES 4

250 ml (9 fl oz/1 cup) coconut milk
1 tablespoon fish sauce
1 tablespoon grated palm (jaggery) sugar
    (see NOTE)
4 boneless, skinless chicken breasts
2 mangoes, thinly sliced
4 spring onions (scallions), sliced
1 handful coriander (cilantro) leaves
45 g (1½ oz/⅓ cup) coarsely chopped roasted
    unsalted macadamia nuts

DRESSING
2 tablespoons oil
1 teaspoon finely grated lime zest
2 tablespoons lime juice

1   Place the coconut milk, fish sauce and palm sugar in a frying pan and bring to the boil, stirring. Reduce the heat, add the chicken and gently simmer, covered, for 10 minutes, or until the chicken is just tender and cooked through. Leave to cool in the coconut liquid, then remove and pour the liquid into a bowl.

2   To make the dressing, put 125 ml (4 fl oz/ ½ cup) of the reserved coconut cooking liquid, the oil, lime zest and juice in a small bowl and whisk to combine. Season to taste with salt and freshly ground black pepper.

3   Cut each chicken breast diagonally into long slices and arrange them with the sliced mango on individual serving plates, or in a large serving bowl. Spoon the dressing over the chicken and mango and top with the spring onion, coriander leaves and macadamia nuts.

NOTE: *Palm (jaggery) sugar is obtained from either the palmyra palm or sugar palm, and is available in block form or in jars. It can be grated or gently melted before using. Soft brown sugar may be substituted.*

NUTRITION PER SERVE
Protein 30 g; Fat 35 g; Carbohydrate 15 g; Dietary
Fibre 2 g; Cholesterol 55 mg; 1965 kJ (465 Cal)

Cut the mangoes into thin slices and carefully remove the skin.

Cut each of the chicken breasts diagonlly into long slices.

Chicken, prawn and grapefruit salad

PREPARATION TIME: 20 MINUTES | TOTAL COOKING TIME: NIL | SERVES 4–6

1 small pink or yellow grapefruit

½ small green papaya or green mango (about 100 g/3½ oz)

6 cooked prawns, peeled and deveined

2 roma (plum) tomatoes, chopped

1 orange, peeled and segmented

125 g (4½ oz) cooked chicken, shredded or cut into bite-sized pieces (see NOTE)

4 spring onions (scallions), sliced

2 garlic cloves, sliced

2 tablespoons chopped coriander (cilantro) leaves

1 tablespoon desiccated coconut

lettuce leaves, to serve

1 tablespoon roasted, unsalted peanuts, finely chopped

DRESSING

2 teaspoons soft brown sugar

1½ tablespoons fish sauce

3 tablespoons lime juice

2 teaspoons chilli sauce

1 Peel the grapefruit, discarding the pith, then cut it into thin segments. Peel the papaya and cut it into long, thin strips.

2 Combine the papaya, grapefruit, prawns, tomato, orange segments, chicken, spring onion, garlic, coriander and coconut in a bowl.

3 To make the dressing, combine all the ingredients in a bowl and whisk until the sugar has dissolved. Pour the dressing over the salad and toss gently. Serve on a bed of lettuce leaves and sprinkle with the peanuts and freshly ground black pepper.

NOTE: *Use leftover chicken, or pan-fry a chicken breast until cooked through and tender.*

NUTRITION PER SERVE (6)
Protein 9.5 g; Fat 1.5 g; Carbohydrate 8.5 g; Dietary Fibre 2.5 g; Cholesterol 34 mg; 376 kJ (98 Cal)

Peel the grapefruit, removing all the white pith. Cut into thin segments.

Using a sharp knife cut the peeled papaya into long, thin strips.

Succulent chicken and pasta salad

PREPARATION TIME: 30 MINUTES | TOTAL COOKING TIME: 25 MINUTES | SERVES 4

1 boneless, skinless chicken breast
375 ml (13 fl oz/1½ cups) chicken stock
350 g (12 oz) fusilli pasta
150 g (5½ oz) asparagus, cut into short lengths
150 g (5½ oz) gruyère cheese, grated
2 spring onions (scallions), thinly sliced

DRESSING
60 ml (2 fl oz/¼ cup) olive oil
60 ml (2 fl oz/¼ cup) lemon juice
½ teaspoon sugar

1   Put the chicken and stock in a frying pan. Bring to the boil, then reduce the heat and poach gently, turning regularly, for 8 minutes, or until tender and cooked through. Remove the chicken, cool and slice thinly.

2   Cook the pasta in a large saucepan of boiling salted water for 10–12 minutes, or until *al dente*. Drain and cool.

3   Cook the asparagus in boiling water for 2 minutes. Drain and place in a bowl of iced water. Drain again. Combine with the chicken, pasta, cheese and sping onions in a large bowl.

4   To make the dressing, whisk the ingredients together. Season to taste with salt and pepper. Add to the salad and toss well. Transfer to a serving bowl and serve.

Pour the stock over the chicken and poach over low heat, turning regularly.

Cook the asparagus pieces in a small pan of boiling water.

NUTRITION PER SERVE
Protein 40 g; Fat 30 g; Carbohydrate 60 g; Dietary Fibre 5 g; Cholesterol 70 mg; 2785 kJ (665 Cal)

Chicken and snow pea salad

PREPARATION TIME: 30 MINUTES I TOTAL COOKING TIME: 15 MINUTES I SERVES 6

150 g (5½ oz) snow peas (mangetouts), trimmed
1 tablespoon oil
20 g (¾ oz) butter
4 boneless, skinless chicken breasts
1 carrot, cut into thin matchsticks
2 celery stalks, cut into thin matchsticks
3 spring onions (scallions), cut into thin
   matchsticks
150 g (5½ oz) button mushrooms, sliced
2 tablespoons flat-leaf (Italian) parsley,
   chopped
1 tablespoon chopped tarragon
150 g (5½ oz) watercress or baby English
   spinach leaves, picked over
2 tablespoons almonds, chopped

DRESSING
60 ml (2 fl oz/¼ cup) extra virgin olive oil
1 tablespoon white wine vinegar
½ teaspoon sugar
60 g (2¼ oz/¼ cup) mayonnaise
2 tablespoons sour cream
1 tablespoon mustard

1 Blanch the snow peas until tender but still crisp. Rinse under cold water and drain well. Cut into strips.

2 Heat the oil and butter in a frying pan, add the chicken and cook for 7 minutes on each side, or until cooked through and well browned. Drain on paper towels. Cut into thin slices. Mix together the carrot, snow peas, chicken, celery, spring onion, mushrooms, parsley and tarragon, and season to taste with salt and pepper.

3 To make the dressing, combine the oil, vinegar and sugar. Stir well, then season. Add the mayonnaise, sour cream and mustard and stir until well blended. Plate the watercress, top with the chicken salad and drizzle with the dressing and chopped almonds.

NUTRITION PER SERVE
Protein 20 g; Fat 25 g; Carbohydrate 5 g; Dietary
Fibre 4 g; Cholesterol 60 mg; 1415 kJ (335 Cal)

Using a small knife, trim the mushrooms and cut into thin slices.

Add the mayonnaise, sour cream and mustard and stir until well blended.

Soups

Chicken and vegetable soup

PREPARATION TIME: 1 HOUR + 30 MINUTES COOLING I TOTAL COOKING TIME: 1 HOUR 25 MINUTES I SERVES 6–8

1.5 kg (2 lb 5 oz) chicken
2 carrots, roughly chopped
2 celery stalks, roughly chopped
1 onion, quartered
1 parsley sprig
2 bay leaves
4 black peppercorns
50 g (1¾ oz) butter
2 tablespoons plain (all-purpose) flour
2 potatoes, chopped
250 g (9 oz) butternut pumpkin (squash),
    cut into bite-sized pieces
2 carrots, extra, cut into thin matchsticks
1 leek, cut into small lengths
3 celery stalks, extra, cut into thin matchsticks
100 g (3½ oz) green beans, cut into short
    lengths, or baby green beans, halved
200 g (7 oz) broccoli, cut into small florets
100 g (3½ oz) sugar snap peas, trimmed
50 g (1¾ oz) English spinach leaves,
    shredded
125 ml (4 fl oz/½ cup) cream
4 tablespoons chopped flat-leaf (Italian)
    parsley

NUTRITION PER SERVE (8)
Protein 50 g; Fat 15 g; Carbohydrate 15 g; Dietary
Fibre 6 g; Cholesterol 130 mg; 1700 kJ (400 Cal)

1   Place the chicken in a large saucepan with the carrot, celery, onion, parsley, bay leaves, 2 teaspoons of salt and the peppercorns. Add 3 litres (101 fl oz/12 cups) of water. Bring to the boil, then reduce the heat and simmer for 1 hour, skimming the surface as required. Allow to cool for at least 30 minutes. Strain through a sieve and reserve the liquid for stock, discard the vegetables.

2   Remove the chicken and allow to cool until it is cool enough to handle. Discard the skin, then cut or pull the flesh from the bones and shred into small pieces. Cover and set the chicken meat aside.

3   Heat the butter in a large saucepan over medium heat and, when foaming, add the flour. Cook, stirring, for 1 minute. Remove from the heat and gradually stir in the stock you made earlier. Return to the heat and bring to the boil, stirring constantly. Add the potato, pumpkin and extra carrot and simmer for 7 minutes. Add the leek, extra celery and beans and simmer for a further 5 minutes. Finally, add the broccoli and sugar snap peas and cook for a further 3 minutes.

4   Just before serving, add the chicken, spinach, cream and chopped parsley. Reheat gently but do not allow the soup to boil. Keep stirring until the spinach has wilted. Season to taste with salt and black pepper. Serve the soup immediately and sprinkle with chopped parsley.

Using a knife, trim the tops from the sugar snap peas, pulling down to remove the string.

Add the parsley sprig and bay leaves to the chicken and vegetables in the pan.

Pour in the cream and stir until the spinach has just wilted.

Chicken noodle soup

PREPARATION TIME: 15 MINUTES + 1 HOUR REFRIGERATION | TOTAL COOKING TIME: 1 HOUR 20 MINUTES | SERVES 4–6

1.25 kg (2 lb 12 oz) chicken wings
2 celery stalks, chopped
1 carrot, chopped
1 onion, chopped
1 bay leaf
1 thyme sprig
4 parsley sprigs
45 g (1½ oz) dried fine egg noodles
1 boneless, skinless chicken breast, finely
  chopped
snipped chives, to serve

1　Rinse the chicken wings and place in a large saucepan with the celery, carrot, onion, bay leaf, thyme, parsley, 1 teaspoon salt and 2 litres (68 fl oz/8 cups) of water. Bring to the boil slowly, skimming the surface as required. Simmer, covered, for 1 hour. Allow to cool slightly, then strain and discard the chicken and the vegetables.

2　Cool the stock further, then cover and refrigerate for at least 1 hour, or until fat forms on the surface of the chilled stock that can be skimmed off with a spoon.

3　Place the stock in a large saucepan and bring to the boil. Gently crush the noodles and add to the soup. Return to the boil and simmer for 8 minutes, or until tender. Add the chopped chicken and simmer for a further 4–5 minutes, or until the chicken is cooked through. Serve topped with the chives.

Using a skimmer or slotted spoon, skim the surface of the stock as required.

Using a spoon, remove the fat that forms on the surface of the chilled stock.

NUTRITION PER SERVE (6)
Protein 45 g; Fat 8 g; Carbohydrate 8 g; Dietary
Fibre 2 g; Cholesterol 135 mg; 1205 kJ (290 Cal)

Mulligatawny

PREPARATION TIME: 30 MINUTES | TOTAL COOKING TIME: 1 HOUR 20 MINUTES | SERVES 6

1 kg (2 lb 4 oz) chicken pieces
2 tablespoons plain (all-purpose) flour
2 teaspoons curry powder
½ teaspoon ground ginger
1 teaspoon ground turmeric
60 g (2¼ oz) butter
12 black peppercorns
6 whole cloves
1.5 litres (52 fl oz/6 cups) chicken stock
1 large apple, peeled, cored and chopped
2 tablespoons lemon juice
125 ml (4 fl oz/½ cup) cream
steamed rice, to serve

1   Trim the chicken pieces of excess fat and sinew. In a bowl, combine the flour, curry powder, ginger and turmeric, and rub the mix into the chicken.

2   Heat the butter in a large saucepan and cook the chicken until lightly browned on all sides. Tie the peppercorns and cloves in a small piece of muslin and add to the pan with the stock. Bring to the boil, then reduce the heat slightly and simmer, covered, for 1 hour. Add the apple and cook for a further 15 minutes.

3   Remove the chicken from the pan and discard the muslin bag. When cool enough to handle, remove the skin and bones from the chicken and finely shred the flesh. Skim any fat from the surface of the soup.

4   Return the chicken to the pan. Stir in the lemon juice and cream, and heat through gently. Serve with rice.

NUTRITION PER SERVE
Protein 25 g; Fat 25 g; Carbohydrate 10 g; Dietary Fibre 1 g; Cholesterol 130 mg; 1405 kJ (440 Cal)

Combine the flour, curry powder, ginger and turmeric in a bowl.

Tie the cloves and peppercorns together in a piece of muslin.

Chicken curry laksa

PREPARATION TIME: 30 MINUTES | TOTAL COOKING TIME: 25 MINUTES | SERVES 4

2 boneless, skinless chicken breasts
1 large onion, roughly chopped
5 cm (2 inch) piece fresh ginger, chopped
8 cm (3 inch) piece galangal, peeled and
    chopped
1 lemongrass stem, white part only, roughly
    chopped
2 garlic cloves
1 red chilli, seeded and chopped
2 teaspoons oil
2 tablespoons mild curry paste
500 ml (17 fl oz/2 cups) chicken stock
60 g (2¼ oz) rice vermicelli
50 g (1¾ oz) dried egg noodles
400 ml (14 fl oz) light coconut milk
10 snow peas (mangetouts), halved
3 spring onions (scallions), finely chopped
90 g (3¼ oz/1 cup) bean sprouts
1 small handful coriander (cilantro) leaves

1 Cut the chicken into bite-sized cubes. Process the onion, ginger, galangal, lemongrass, garlic and chilli in a food processor until finely chopped. Add the oil and process until the mixture is a paste-like consistency. Spoon into a large wok, add the curry paste and stir over low heat for 1–2 minutes, or until aromatic. Take care not to burn the mixture.

2 Increase the heat to medium, add the chicken and stir for 2 minutes, or until the chicken is well coated. Stir in the chicken stock and mix well. Bring slowly to the boil, then simmer for 10 minutes, or until the chicken is cooked through.

3 Meanwhile, cut the vermicelli into shorter lengths using scissors—this makes them easier to eat. Cook the vermicelli and egg noodles separately in large saucepans of boiling water for 5 minutes each. Drain and rinse under cold water.

4 Just prior to serving, add the coconut milk and snow peas to the chicken mixture and heat through. To serve, divide the vermicelli and egg noodles among four warmed serving bowls. Pour the hot laksa over the top and garnish with the spring onion, bean sprouts and coriander leaves.

HINT: *If you prefer a more fiery laksa, use a medium or hot brand of curry paste or increase the amount of chilli. Stir the curry paste into the onion mixture, over low heat, until aromatic.*

NUTRITION PER SERVE
Protein 30 g; Fat 8 g; Carbohydrate 4.5 g; Dietary Fibre 3 g; Cholesterol 65 mg; 945 kJ (225 Cal)

Stir the curry paste into the onion mixture, over low heat, until aromatic.

Just before serving, stir the coconut milk into the chicken mixture until heated.

Thai-style chicken and baby corn soup

PREPARATION TIME: 30 MINUTES I TOTAL COOKING TIME: 15 MINUTES I SERVES 4

150 g (5½ oz) whole baby corn (see NOTE)
1 tablespoon oil
2 lemongrass stems, white part only, very
    thinly sliced
2 tablespoons finely grated fresh ginger
6 spring onions (scallions), chopped
1 red chilli, finely chopped
1 litre (35 fl oz/4 cups) chicken stock
375 ml (13 fl oz/1½ cups) coconut milk
2 boneless, skinless chicken breasts,
    thinly sliced
130 g (4½ oz) creamed corn
1 tablespoon soy sauce
2 tablespoons finely snipped chives,
    to serve
1 red chilli, thinly sliced, to serve

1 Cut the baby corn in half or quarters
lengthways, depending on their size.

2 Heat the oil in a saucepan over medium heat.
Cook the lemongrass, ginger, spring onion and
chilli for 1 minute, stirring. Add the stock and
coconut milk and bring to the boil—do not
cover or the coconut milk will curdle.

3 Stir in the corn, chicken and creamed corn
and simmer for 8 minutes, or until the corn
and chicken are just tender. Add the soy sauce,
season well and serve garnished with the chives
and chilli.

NOTE: *Tinned baby corn can be substituted
for fresh corn. Add during the last 2 minutes
of cooking.*

Grate the peeled ginger, using the fine side of
the grater.

Cut the baby corn lengthways into halves or
quarters, depending on size.

NUTRITION PER SERVE
Protein 20 g; Fat 25 g; Carbohydrate 15 g; Dietary
Fibre 3 g; Cholesterol 30 mg; 1520 kJ (360 Cal)

Lemon chicken soup

PREPARATION TIME: 10 MINUTES | TOTAL COOKING TIME: 10 MINUTES | SERVES 4

2 boneless, skinless chicken breasts
1 lemon
1 litre (35 fl oz/4 cups) chicken stock
2 lemon thyme sprigs, plus extra, to serve
   (see NOTE)

1 Trim any excess fat from the chicken. Using a vegetable peeler, cut 3 strips of zest from the lemon and remove the pith. Place the stock, 2 strips of zest and lemon thyme in a shallow saucepan and slowly bring almost to the boil. Reduce the heat to simmering point, add the chicken and cook, covered, for 7 minutes, or until the meat is cooked through. Meanwhile, cut the remaining zest into very fine strips.

2 Remove the chicken from the pan, transfer to a plate and cover with foil.

3 Strain the stock into a clean pan through a sieve lined with 2 layers of damp muslin. Finely shred the chicken and return to the soup. Reheat gently and season to taste with salt and black pepper. Serve immediately, garnished with the extra sprigs of lemon thyme and lemon zest.

NOTE: *You can use ordinary thyme if lemon thyme is not available.*

NUTRITION PER SERVE
Protein 25 g; Fat 3 g; Carbohydrate 0 g; Dietary
Fibre 0 g; Cholesterol 55 mg; 535 kJ (130 Cal)

Using a small knife, remove the white pith from the lemon zest.

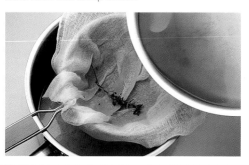

Strain the stock into a clean saucepan through a sieve lined with damp muslin.

Finely shred the chicken into thin pieces and return to the soup.

Herbed chicken soup

PREPARATION TIME: 30 MINUTES | TOTAL COOKING TIME: 30 MINUTES | SERVES 6

1 boneless, skinless chicken breast
1 bay leaf
6 black peppercorns
1 whole clove
4 parsley sprigs
2 tablespoons olive oil
1 onion, finely chopped
1 small carrot, finely chopped
1 celery stalk, finely chopped
1 large potato, finely chopped
1 teaspoon finely chopped rosemary,
    or ¼ teaspoon dried
1 teaspoon chopped thyme,
    or ½ teaspoon dried
1 teaspoon chopped marjoram,
    or ½ teaspoon dried
1 litre (35 fl oz/4 cups) chicken stock
310 g (11 oz) tinned creamed corn
4 tablespoons finely chopped flat-leaf
    (Italian) parsley

1   Trim the chicken breast of excess fat and sinew. Put 500 ml (17 fl oz/2 cups) water in a saucepan and bring to a simmer. Add the chicken, bay leaf, peppercorns, clove and parsley and cook for 8 minutes, or until the chicken is tender and cooked through. Remove the chicken from the liquid and cool slightly before shredding. Discard the bay leaf, peppercorns, clove and parsley, and reserve the cooking liquid.

2   Heat the oil in a large, heavy-based saucepan. Add the onion, carrot and celery and cook over medium heat for 5 minutes, or until the onion is soft. Add the potato, rosemary, thyme and marjoram and cook, stirring, over medium heat for 1 minute.

3   Add the stock and reserved cooking liquid. Season to taste with salt and pepper and bring to the boil. Reduce the heat and simmer for 15 minutes, or until the potato and carrot have softened. Add the creamed corn and shredded chicken and stir for 2 minutes, or until heated through. Stir in the parsley.

HINT: *Use shredded barbecued chicken if you prefer—add extra stock to make up the liquid.*

NUTRITION PER SERVE
Protein 11 g; Fat 7.5 g; Carbohydrate 15 g; Dietary Fibre 3 g; Cholesterol 18 mg; 695 kJ (166 Cal)

Simmer the chicken breast with the bay leaf, peppercorns, clove and parsley until cooked.

Add the potato and herbs to the vegetable mixture and cook over medium heat.

Add the shredded chicken and creamed corn to the soup.

Cock-a-leekie

PREPARATION TIME: 10 MINUTES + 2 HOURS REFRIGERATION | TOTAL COOKING TIME: 1 HOUR 40 MINUTES | SERVES 4–6

1.5 kg (3 lb 5 oz) chicken
250 g (9 oz) chicken giblets, optional
1 onion, sliced
2 litres (70 fl oz/8 cups) chicken stock
4 leeks, thinly sliced
¼ teaspoon ground coriander
pinch nutmeg
bouquet garni
12 pitted prunes
pinch cayenne pepper
3 thyme sprigs, plus extra, to serve

1   Put the chicken in a large saucepan and add the giblets (if using), onion and stock. Bring to the boil, skimming the surface as required. Add the leek, coriander, nutmeg and bouquet garni. Reduce the heat, cover and simmer for 1¼ hours.

2   Remove the chicken and bouquet garni from the pan and lift out the giblets with a slotted spoon. Cool the stock, then refrigerate for 2 hours. Spoon off the fat from the surface and discard. Remove the chicken meat from the bones and shred. Discard the skin and carcass.

3   Return the chicken to the soup with the prunes, cayenne pepper and thyme. Simmer for 20 minutes. Season to taste and garnish with the extra thyme sprigs.

NUTRITION PER SERVE (6)
Protein 60 g; Fat 6 g; Carbohydrate 7 g; Dietary Fibre 1 g; Cholesterol 125 mg; 1310 kJ (315 Cal)

Wrap the thyme, parsley and bay leaves in a small square of muslin.

Add the chicken stock to the saucepan with the chicken, giblets (if using) and onion.

Add the cayenne pepper, prunes and thyme sprigs to the soup and stir to combine.

Chinese mushroom and chicken soup

PREPARATION TIME: 20 MINUTES + 10 MINUTES SOAKING | TOTAL COOKING TIME: 10 MINUTES | SERVES 4

3 dried Chinese mushrooms
185 g (6½ oz) thin dried egg noodles
1 tablespoon oil
4 spring onions (scallions), cut into thin
    matchsticks
1 tablespoon soy sauce
2 tablespoons rice wine, mirin or sherry
(see NOTE)
1.25 litres (44 fl oz/5 cups) chicken stock
½ small barbecued chicken, shredded
50 g (1¾ oz) sliced ham, cut into strips
90 g (3¼ oz/1 cup) bean sprouts
coriander (cilantro) leaves, to serve
thinly sliced red chilli, to serve

1 Soak the mushrooms in boiling water for
10 minutes. Drain, then squeeze to remove the
excess liquid. Remove the stems and thinkly slice
the caps.

2 Cook the noodles in a large saucepan of
boiling water for 3 minutes, or according to the
manufacturer's directions. Drain and cut the
noodles into shorter lengths with scissors.

3 Heat the oil in a large heavy-based pan. Add
the mushrooms and spring onion. Cook for
1 minute, then add the soy sauce, rice wine and
stock. Bring slowly to the boil and cook for
1 minute. Reduce the heat then add the noodles,
shredded chicken, ham and bean sprouts. Heat
through for 2 minutes without allowing the soup
to boil.

4 Use tongs to divide the noodles among
four bowls, ladle in the remaining mixture, and
garnish with coriander leaves and sliced chilli.

NOTE: *Rice wine and mirin are available at
Asian food stores.*

NUTRITION PER SERVE
Protein 25 g; Fat 10 g; Carbohydrate 35 g; Dietary
Fibre 3 g; Cholesterol 80 mg; 1426 kJ (340 cal)

Put the mushrooms in a bowl, cover with boiling
water and leave to soak.

Cut the noodles into shorter lengths to make them
easier to eat.

Spicy chicken broth with coriander pasta

PREPARATION TIME: 40 MINUTES | TOTAL COOKING TIME: 50 MINUTES | SERVES 4

350 g (12 oz) boneless, skinless chicken
    thighs or wings
2 carrots, finely chopped
2 celery stalks, finely chopped
2 small leeks, finely chopped
3 egg whites
1.5 litres (52 fl oz/6 cups) chicken stock
Tabasco sauce

CORIANDER PASTA
60 g (2¼ oz/½ cup) plain (all-purpose) flour
1 egg
½ teaspoon sesame oil
1 large handful coriander (cilantro) leaves

1 Put the chicken, carrot, celery and leek in a large saucepan. Push the chicken to one side and add the egg whites to the vegetables. Using a wire whisk, beat until frothy (take care not to use a pan that can be scratched by the whisk).

2 Warm the stock in another saucepan, then add gradually to the first pan, whisking constantly to froth the egg whites. Continue whisking while slowly bringing to the boil. Make a hole in the top of the froth with a spoon and leave to simmer, uncovered, for 30 minutes without stirring. Line a strainer with a damp tea towel (dish towel) and strain the broth into a bowl. Discard the chicken and vegetables. Season to taste with salt, pepper and Tabasco. Set aside.

3 To make the coriander pasta, sift the flour into a bowl and make a well in the centre. Whisk the egg and oil together and pour into the well. Mix to a soft dough and knead on a floured surface for 2 minutes, or until smooth.

4 Divide the pasta dough into four even portions. Roll one portion out very thinly (best to use a pasta mashine) and cover with a layer of evenly spaced coriander leaves. Roll out another portion of pasta and lay this on top of the leaves. Repeat with the remaining pasta and coriander.

5 Cut squares of pasta around the coriander leaves. Bring the chicken broth gently to a simmer. Add the pasta, cook for 1 minute and serve.

NUTRITION PER SERVE
Protein 23 g; Fat 4 g; Carbohydrate 17 g; Dietary Fibre 3 g; Cholesterol 80 mg; 832 kJ (200 Cal)

Use a metal spoon to make a hole in the froth on top of the soup to prevent the stock from boiling over.

Strain the broth through a damp tea towel or double thickness of muslin.

Cut out neat squares of the pasta around each coriander leaf.

Tom kha gai (chicken and coconut soup)

PREPARATION TIME: 20 MINUTES | TOTAL COOKING TIME: 20 MINUTES | SERVES 4

5 cm (2 inch) piece galangal (see HINT)
500 ml (17 fl oz/2 cups) coconut milk
250 ml (9 fl oz/1 cup) chicken stock
3 boneless, skinless chicken breasts, cut into
thin strips
1–2 teaspoons finely chopped red chilli
2 tablespoons fish sauce
1 teaspoon soft brown sugar
1 small handful coriander (cilantro) leaves

1 Peel the galangal and cut it into thin slices. Combine the galangal, coconut milk and stock in a medium saucepan. Bring to the boil and simmer, uncovered, over low heat for 10 minutes, stirring occasionally.

2 Add the chicken strips and chilli to the pan and simmer for 8 minutes.

3 Stir in the fish sauce and brown sugar. Add the coriander leaves and serve immediately.

HINT: *If fresh galangal is not available, you can use 5 large slices of dried galangal instead. Prepare by soaking the slices in a little boiling water for 10 minutes and then cutting them into shreds. Add the soaking liquid to the chicken stock to make 250 ml (9 fl oz/1 cup) and use it in the recipe.*

Break the galangal so you have a piece measuring about 5 cm (2 inches).

Add the chicken strips and chilli to the simmering coconut milk mixture.

NUTRITION PER SERVE
Protein 40 g; Fat 30 g; Carbohydrate 6.5 g; Dietary Fibre 2.5 g; Cholesterol 83 mg; 1876 kJ (448 Cal)

Asian chicken and noodle soup

PREPARATION TIME: 20 MINUTES | TOTAL COOKING TIME: 25 MINUTES | SERVES 4

CHILLI PASTE
4 dried chillies, roughly chopped
1 teaspoon coriander seeds
1 teaspoon grated fresh ginger
1 spring onion (scallion), chopped
½ teaspoon ground turmeric

750 ml (26 fl oz/3 cups) coconut milk
350 g (12 oz) boneless, skinless chicken breast,
    thinly sliced
2 tablespoons soy sauce
500 ml (17 fl oz/2 cups) chicken stock
400 g (14 oz) dried egg noodles
peanut oil, for deep-frying
spring onion (scallion), to serve
red chillies, to serve

1 To make the chilli paste, put all the ingredients in a small saucepan. Stir over low heat for 5 minutes, or until fragrant. Transfer to a mortar and pestle or food processor and grind until smooth.

2 Heat 250 ml (9 fl oz/1 cup) of the coconut milk in a saucepan. Add the chilli paste and stir for 2–3 minutes. Add the chicken and soy sauce and cook for 3–4 minutes. Stir in the remaining coconut milk and the stock. Bring to the boil, reduce the heat and simmer for 10 minutes.

3 Break a quarter of the noodles into large pieces. Fry in the hot peanut oil until crisp, then drain on paper towels. Cook the remaining noodles in boiling water until just tender, then drain.

4 Place the boiled noodles in serving bowls and ladle the soup over the top. Garnish with the fried noodles and serve with spring onion and chilli.

Grind the spices for the chilli paste in a mortar and pestle.

Fry a quarter of the noodles in hot peanut oil until crisp. Drain on paper towels.

NUTRITION PER SERVE
Protein 35 g; Fat 35 g; Carbohydrate 75 g; Dietary Fibre 3 g; Cholesterol 60 mg; 2025 kJ (480 Cal)

Roasted capsicum and smoked chicken soup

PREPARATION TIME: 20 MINUTES | TOTAL COOKING TIME: 30 MINUTES | SERVES 6–8

4 large red capsicums (peppers)
1 long green chilli
1 tablespoon olive oil
1 large onion, roughly chopped
2 garlic cloves, crushed
½ teaspoon cayenne pepper
1 teaspoon ground coriander
1 teaspoon ground cumin
2 litres (68 fl oz/8 cups) chicken stock
315 g (61 oz) smoked chicken, cubed
1 handfull coriander (cilantro) leaves
sour cream and tortilla chips, to serve

NUTRITION PER SERVE (8)
Protein 35 g; Fat 30 g; Carbohydrate 20 g; Dietary
Fibre 5 g; Cholesterol 155 mg; 2120 kJ (505 Cal)

1 Remove the seeds and membrane from the capsicums and the chilli, and cut into large flattish pieces. Cook, skin-side-up, under a hot grill (broiler) until the skin blackens and blisters. Remove from the heat, place in a plastic bag and leave to cool, then peel away the skin. Roughly chop the capsicum, and finely slice the chilli.

2 Heat the olive oil in a large saucepan over medium heat. Add the onion and garlic, and fry for 2–3 minutes. Mix in the cayenne pepper, coriander and cumin and cook for a further 1 minute, stirring constantly. Add the stock, roasted capsicum and chilli and bring to the boil. Reduce the heat and simmer gently for 15 minutes.

3 Remove from the heat, leave to cool slightly, then purée in a blender or food processor in batches until it becomes a smooth soup. Return the soup to the pan.

4 Reheat the soup over medium heat for 10 minutes. Stir in the chicken and season with pepper. When the soup is hot and ready to serve, add the coriander leaves. Ladle the soup into serving bowls and top each with sour cream. Serve with the tortilla chips.

When the capsicum has cooled, peel away the blackened skin with your fingers.

Add the stock, roasted chopped capsicum and chilli to the pan.

Transfer the mixture to a food processor in batches and purée until smooth.

Creamy spinach and chicken soup

PREPARATION TIME: 40 MINUTES I TOTAL COOKING TIME: 55 MINUTES I SERVES 6

1 tablespoon oil
1 kg (2 lb/4 oz) chicken pieces
1 carrot, chopped
2 celery stalks, chopped
1 onion, chopped
6 black peppercorns
2 garlic cloves, chopped
bouquet garni
800 g (1 lb 12 oz) sweet potato, chopped
500 g (1 lb/2 oz) English spinach
125 ml (4 fl oz/½ cup) cream

1 Heat the oil in a large saucepan, add the chicken pieces in batches and brown well. Drain on paper towels. Pour off the excess fat, leaving 1 tablespoon in the pan. Return the chicken to the pan with the carrot, celery, onion, peppercorns, garlic, bouquet garni and 1.5 litres (52 fl oz/6 cups) of water.

2 Bring the soup to the boil, reduce the heat and simmer for 40 minutes. Strain, discarding the vegetables, peppercorns and bouquet garni. Return the stock to the pan. Pull the chicken meat from the bones, shred and set aside.

3 Add the sweet potato to the stock in the pan. Bring to the boil, then reduce the heat and simmer until tender. Add the spinach leaves and cook until wilted. Process the spinach in batches in a food processor until finely chopped.

4 Return the spinach to the pan, add the shredded chicken and stir in the cream. Season to taste. Reheat gently before serving but do not allow the soup to boil.

To make a bouquet garni, tie parsley, thyme and a bay leaf with string.

Add the spinach leaves to the soup and cook, stirring, until just wilted.

NUTRITION PER SERVE
Protein 40 g; Fat 15 g; Carbohydrate 25 g; Dietary Fibre 4 g; Cholesterol 110 mg; 1720 kJ (410 Cal)

Chicken and couscous soup

PREPARATION TIME: 25 MINUTES | TOTAL COOKING TIME: 30 MINUTES | SERVES 6

1 tablespoon olive oil
1 onion, sliced
½ teaspoon ground cumin
½ teaspoon paprika
1 teaspoon grated fresh ginger
1 garlic clove, crushed
2 celery stalks, sliced
2 small carrots, sliced
2 zucchini (courgettes), sliced
1.25 litres (44 fl oz/5 cups) chicken stock
2 boneless, skinless chicken breasts, sliced
pinch saffron threads, optional
95 g (3¼ oz/½ cup) instant couscous
2 tablespoons chopped flat-leaf (Italian)
    parsley

1   Heat the oil in a large heavy-based saucepan.
Add the onion and cook over medium heat
for 10 minutes, or until very soft, stirring
occasionally. Add the cumin, paprika, ginger and
garlic and cook, stirring, for 1 minute further.

2   Add the celery, carrot and zucchini and stir
to coat with the spices. Stir in the stock. Bring
to the boil, then reduce the heat and simmer,
partially covered, for about 15 minutes, or until
the vegetables are tender.

3   Add the chicken and saffron to the pan and
cook for about 5 minutes, or until the chicken is
just tender; do not overcook. Stir in the couscous
and chopped parsley and serve.

HINT: *Add the couscous to the soup just before
serving because it absorbs liquid quickly and
becomes very thick.*

NUTRITION PER SERVE
Protein 19 g; Fat 5.5 g; Carbohydrate 12 g; Dietary
Fibre 2 g; Cholesterol 37 mg; 712 kJ (170 Cal)

Stir the chicken and saffron threads into the
soup mixture.

Do not stir in the parsley and couscous until just
before the soup is served.

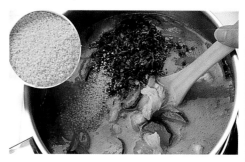

Curries
and stir-fries

Sichuan pepper chicken stir-fry

PREPARATION TIME: 25 MINUTES + 2 HOURS MARINATING | TOTAL COOKING TIME: 20 MINUTES | SERVES 4

3 teaspoons sichuan peppercorns

500 g (1 lb/2 oz) boneless, skinless chicken
    thighs, cut into strips

2 tablespoons soy sauce

1 garlic clove, crushed

1 teaspoon grated fresh ginger

3 teaspoons cornflour (cornstarch)

100 g (3½ oz) dried thin egg noodles

oil, for cooking

1 onion, sliced

1 yellow capsicum (pepper), cut into
    thin strips

1 red capsicum (pepper), cut into thin strips

100 g (3½ oz) sugar snap peas

60 ml (2 fl oz/¼ cup) chicken stock

NUTRITION PER SERVE
Protein 35 g; Fat 15 g; Carbohydrate 25 g; Dietary
Fibre 3 g; Cholesterol 65 mg; 1515 kJ (360 Cal)

1 Heat a wok until very hot and dry-fry the sichuan peppercorns for 30 seconds. Remove from the wok and crush with a mortar and pestle or in a spice mill or small food processor.

2 Combine the chicken pieces with the soy sauce, garlic, ginger, cornflour and sichuan pepper in a glass or ceramic bowl. Cover and refrigerate for 2 hours.

3 Bring a large saucepan of water to the boil, add the egg noodles and cook for 5 minutes, or until tender. Drain, then drizzle with a little oil and toss it through the noodles to prevent them from sticking together. Set aside.

4 Heat the wok until very hot, add 1 tablespoon of the oil and swirl it around to coat the side. Stir-fry the chicken in batches over medium–high heat for 5 minutes, or until golden brown and cooked. Add more oil when necessary. Remove from the wok and set aside.

5 Reheat the wok, add 1 tablespoon of the oil and stir-fry the onion, capsicum and sugar snap peas over high heat for 2–3 minutes, or until the vegetables are tender. Add the chicken stock and bring to the boil.

6 Return the chicken and egg noodles to the wok and toss over high heat until the mixture is well combined. Serve immediately.

Heat the wok until very hot, then dry-fry the sichuan peppercorns.

Crush the sichuan peppercorns with a mortar and pestle.

Toss the oil through the noodles to prevent them from sticking.

Lemon chicken

PREPARATION TIME: 15 MINUTES + 30 MINUTES MARINATING | TOTAL COOKING TIME: 10 MINUTES | SERVES 4

3 boneless, skinless chicken breasts
1 egg white, lightly beaten
2 teaspoons cornflour (cornstarch)
¼ teaspoon grated fresh ginger
60 ml (2 fl oz/¼ cup) oil

LEMON SAUCE
2 teaspoons cornflour (cornstarch)
1½ tablespoons caster (superfine) sugar
2 tablespoons lemon juice
185 ml (6 fl oz/¾ cup) chicken stock
2 teaspoons soy sauce
1 teaspoon dry sherry

1   Pat the chicken dry with paper towels. Cut the chicken breasts on the diagonal into 1 cm (½ inch) wide strips. Combine the egg white, cornflour, ginger and ½ teaspoon of salt. Add the chicken strips, mixing well. Marinate in the refrigerator for 30 minutes.

2   Heat the oil in a wok or heavy-based frying pan, swirling to coat the side. Drain the chicken from the marinade, add to the pan and stir-fry over medium–high heat for 5 minutes or until just cooked but not browned. Place the chicken on a plate to keep warm while preparing the sauce. Carefully pour the excess oil from the wok and discard.

3   To make the lemon sauce, mix the cornflour with 2 tablespoons water to form a smooth paste. Add to the wok with the remaining ingredients. Stir over high heat and boil for 1 minute. Add the chicken, stirring to coat it with the sauce. Transfer to a serving platter. Serve immediately with steamed rice and stir-fried vegetables.

Stir-fry the marinated chicken until it is just cooked but not browned.

Add the cornflour mixture to the wok with the sugar, lemon juice, stock, soy sauce and sherry.

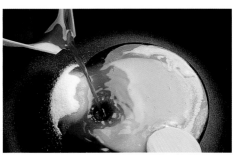

NUTRITION PER SERVE
Protein 29 g; Fat 17 g; Carbohydrate 8 g; Dietary Fibre 0 g; Cholesterol 63 mg; 1280 kJ (306 Cal)

Chicken with oyster sauce and basil

PREPARATION TIME: 20 MINUTES | TOTAL COOKING TIME: 10 MINUTES | SERVES 4

60 ml (2 fl oz/ ¼ cup) oyster sauce
2 tablespoons fish sauce
1 tablespoon grated palm (jaggery) sugar
1 tablespoon oil
2–3 garlic cloves, crushed
1 tablespoon grated fresh ginger
1–2 red chillies, seeded and finely chopped
4 spring onions (scallions), finely chopped
1 boneless, skinless chicken breast, cut into
    thin strips
250 g (9 oz) broccoli, cut into florets
230 g (8 oz) tinned water chestnuts, drained
230 g (8 oz) tinned sliced bamboo
    shoots, rinsed
1 handful basil, shredded

1 Put 60 ml (2 fl oz/¼ cup) water in a small
bowl with the oyster sauce, fish sauce and palm
sugar. Mix well.

2 Heat a wok until very hot, add the oil and
swirl it around to coat the side. Stir-fry the garlic,
ginger, chilli and spring onion for 1 minute over
medium heat. Increase the heat to high, add the
chicken and stir-fry for 2–3 minutes, or until it is
just cooked. Remove from the wok.

3 Reheat the wok and add the broccoli, water
chestnuts and bamboo shoots. Stir-fry for 2–3
minutes, tossing constantly. Add the sauce and
bring to the boil, tossing constantly. Return the
chicken to the wok and toss until it is heated
through. Stir in the basil and serve immediately.

NUTRITION PER SERVE
Protein 30 g; Fat 3.5 g; Carbohydrate 35 g; Dietary
Fibre 8 g; Cholesterol 45 mg; 1205 KJ 285 Cal)

Crush the palm sugar with the back of a
large knife.

Remove the seeds from the chillies and chop the
chillies finely.

Chicken donburi

PREPARATION TIME: 35 MINUTES | TOTAL COOKING TIME: 30 MINUTES | SERVES 4

440 g (15½ oz/2 cups) short-grain rice
2 tablespoons oil
250 g (9 oz) boneless, skinless chicken
    breasts, cut into thin strips
2 onions, thinly sliced
80 ml (2½ fl oz/⅓ cup) shoyu
    (Japanese soy sauce)
2 tablespoons mirin
1 teaspoon dashi granules
5 eggs, lightly beaten
2 nori sheets
2 spring onions (scallions), sliced

1 Wash the rice in a colander under cold running water until the water runs clear. Transfer the rice to a heavy-based saucepan, add 600 ml (21 fl oz) water and bring to the boil over high heat. Cover the pan with a tight-fitting lid and reduce the heat to as low as possible (otherwise the rice in the bottom of the pan will burn) and cook for 15 minutes. Turn the heat to very high, for 15–20 seconds, remove the pan from the heat and set aside for 12 minutes, without lifting the lid or the steam will escape.

2 Heat the oil in a frying pan over high heat. Add the chicken and stir-fry until tender. Remove the chicken from the pan and set aside. Reheat the pan, add the onion and cook, stirring occasionally, for 3 minutes, or until beginning to soften. Add 80 ml (2½ fl oz/ ⅓ cup) water, the shoyu, mirin and dashi granules. Stir to dissolve the dashi, and bring to the boil. Cook for 3 minutes, or until the onion is tender.

3 Return the chicken to the pan and pour in the egg, stirring gently to break up. Cover and simmer over very low heat for 2–3 minutes, or until the egg is just set. Remove the pan from the heat. To make the nori crisp, hold it over low heat, moving it back and forward for about 15 seconds, then crumble it into small pieces.

4 Transfer the rice to a serving dish, carefully spoon over the chicken and egg mixture and sprinkle with the crumbled nori. Garnish with the spring onion.

NUTRITION PER SERVE
Protein 32 g; Fat 18 g; Carbohydrate 90 g; Dietary Fibre 3.6 g; Cholesterol 256 mg; 2737 kJ (654 Cal)

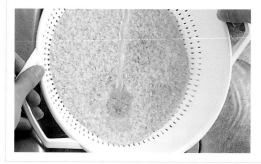

Wash the rice well in a colander under cold running water until the water runs clear.

Cook the onion for about 3 minutes, or until it begins to soften.

Pour the egg into the pan and stir gently to break it up.

Goan-style chicken with sultanas and almonds

PREPARATION TIME: 20 MINUTES | TOTAL COOKING TIME: 20 MINUTES | SERVES 3–4

2 teaspoons ground cumin
2 teaspoons ground coriander
1 teaspoon ground cinnamon
½ teaspoon cayenne pepper
½ teaspoon ground cardamom
oil, for cooking
1 large onion, cut into thin wedges
2 garlic cloves, finely chopped
500 g (1 lb/2 oz) boneless, skinless chicken
    breasts, cut into cubes
2 teaspoons finely grated orange zest
2 tablespoons orange juice
2 tablespoons sultanas (golden raisins)
1 teaspoon soft brown sugar
60 g (2¼ oz/¼ cup) thick plain yoghurt
40 g (1½ oz/⅓ cup) slivered almonds, toasted

1 Dry-fry the spices in a wok over low heat for about 1 minute, or until fragrant, shaking the wok regularly.

2 Add 1 tablespoon oil to the wok and stir-fry the onion wedges and garlic over high heat for 3 minutes. Remove from the wok.

3 Reheat the wok, add 1 tablespoon of the oil and stir-fry the chicken in two batches until it is golden and just cooked. Return all the chicken to the wok with the onion mixture, orange zest, juice, sultanas and sugar. Cook for 1 minute, tossing until most of the juice evaporates.

4 Stir in the yoghurt and reheat gently, without boiling or the yoghurt will separate. Season well with salt and pepper. Serve garnished with the toasted almonds.

NOTE: *Yoghurt separates easily when heated due to its acid balance. Yoghurt also separates when shaken, whipped or stirred too much.*

Toast the almonds by dry-frying them in the wok until golden brown.

Add the onion mixture, orange zest, juice, sultanas and sugar to the chicken.

NUTRITION PER SERVE (4)
Protein 30 g; Fat 20 g; Carbohydrate 15 g; Dietary Fibre 2.5 g; Cholesterol 65 mg; 1500 kJ (360 Cal)

Chicken and lime curry

PREPARATION TIME: 30 MINUTES | TOTAL COOKING TIME: 45 MINUTES | SERVES 4

SPICE PASTE
1 large onion, roughly chopped
6 red chillies, seeded and finely chopped
4 garlic cloves, crushed
1 teaspoon finely chopped lemongrass, white
    part only
2 teaspoons finely chopped fresh galangal
1 teaspoon ground turmeric

1.6 kg (3 lb/8 oz) chicken
60 ml (2 fl oz/¼ cup) oil
250 ml (9 fl oz/1 cup) coconut milk
2 limes, halved
5 makrut (kaffir lime) leaves, finely shredded
1 tablespoon fish sauce
2 limes, quartered, extra to serve

1 To make the spice paste, finely chop all the ingredients in a food processor for a few minutes, or until the mixture is a rough, thick paste.

2 Cut the chicken through the bone into large bite-sized pieces. Heat the oil in a large heavy-based saucepan or wok and add the spice paste. Cook over low heat, stirring occasionally, for 10 minutes, or until fragrant.

3 Add the chicken and stir-fry for 2 minutes, making sure the pieces are well covered with the spice paste. Add the coconut milk, 125 ml (4 fl oz/½ cup) water, lime halves and shredded makrut leaves. Simmer the mixture for 20–25 minutes, or until the chicken is tender, and cooked through, stirring regularly.

4 Discard the limes. Add the fish sauce, and serve with the extra lime wedges and steamed rice.

Finely shred the makrut leaves with a sharp kitchen knife.

Season the curry with 1 tablespoon of fish sauce before serving.

Butter chicken

PREPARATION TIME: 30 MINUTES + 4 HOURS MARINATING | TOTAL COOKING TIME: 25 MINUTES | SERVES 4

1 kg (2 lb/4 oz) boneless, skinless
    chicken thighs
60 ml (2 fl oz/¼ cup) lemon juice
250 g (9 oz/1 cup) yoghurt
1 onion, chopped
2 garlic cloves, crushed
3 cm (1¼ inch) piece fresh ginger, grated
1 green chilli, chopped
3 teaspoons garam masala
125 ml (4 fl oz/½ cup) tomato paste
    (concentrated purée)
2 cm (¾ inch) piece fresh ginger, extra, finely
    grated
250 ml (9 fl oz/1 cup) cream
2 teaspoons sugar
¼ teaspoon chilli powder
1 tablespoon lemon juice, extra
1 teaspoon ground cumin
100 g (3½ oz) butter
1 makrut (kaffir lime) leaf, shredded,
    to garnish

NUTRITION PER SERVE
Protein 55 g; Fat 60 g; Carbohydrate 10 g; Dietary
Fibre 2 g; Cholesterol 330 mg; 3390 kJ (805 Cal)

1 Cut the chicken into 2 cm (¾ inch) thick strips. Sprinkle with 1 teaspoon of salt and the lemon juice.

2 Place the yoghurt, onion, garlic, ginger, chilli and 2 teaspoons of the garam masala in a food processor and blend until smooth.

3 Place the chicken strips in a non-metallic dish. Add the yoghurt mixture and toss to combine. Cover and refrigerate for 4 hours. Remove the chicken from the marinade and allow to drain for 5 minutes.

4 Preheat the oven to 220°C (425°F/Gas 7). Place the chicken in a shallow baking dish and bake for 15 minutes, or until it is tender. Drain off any excess juice, cover loosely with foil and keep warm.

5 Mix together the tomato paste and 125 ml (4 fl oz/½ cup) water in a large bowl. Add the ginger, cream, remaining garam marsala, sugar, chilli powder, lemon juice and cumin, and stir to thoroughly combine.

6 Melt the butter in a large saucepan over medium heat. Stir in the tomato mixture and bring to the boil. Cook for 2 minutes, then reduce the heat and add the chicken pieces. Stir to coat the chicken with the sauce and simmer for a further 2 minutes, or until completely heated through. Serve with rice and garnish with some shredded makrut leaves.

Sprinkle the salt and pour the lemon juice over the chicken strips.

Process the yoghurt, onion, garlic, ginger, chilli and garam masala.

Add the chicken pieces to the saucepan and stir to coat with the sauce.

Chicken with creamy curry sauce

PREPARATION TIME: 25 MINUTES I TOTAL COOKING TIME: 40 MINUTES I SERVES 4

1 tablespoon oil
50 g (1¾ oz) butter
1 onion, chopped
2 garlic cloves, crushed
2 teaspoons grated fresh ginger
1 green chilli, seeded and finely chopped
¼ teaspoon crushed cardamom seeds
1 teaspoon garam masala
1 teaspoon ground turmeric
1 tablespoon plain (all-purpose) flour
375 ml (13 fl oz/1½ cups) chicken stock
80 ml (2½ fl oz/⅓ cup) brandy
125 ml (4 fl oz/½ cup) cream
4 large boneless, skinless chicken breasts,
    each cut into thirds and flattened with
    a meat mallet
flaked toasted almonds, to serve
chopped coriander (cilantro) leaves, to serve

1   Heat the oil and half the butter in a large, deep frying pan. Add the onion and cook over medium heat until soft and transparent. Add the garlic, ginger and chilli and cook for 1 minute. Add the cardamom, garam masala and turmeric and cook for 1 minute. Stir in the flour and cook for 1 minute.

2   Remove from the heat. Gradually mix in the combined chicken stock, brandy and cream, stirring constantly. Return to the heat. Cook, stirring, until the sauce boils and thickens. Cover and simmer over low heat for 15 minutes.

3   Meanwhile, heat the remaining butter in a frying pan and brown the chicken pieces. Add the chicken to the sauce and cook for a further 10–15 minutes to reduce. Season to taste with salt and pepper. Serve scattered with toasted almonds and coriander.

Seed and finely chop the green chilli with a sharp knife.

Gradually add the combined stock, brandy and cream, stirring constantly.

NUTRITION PER SERVE
Protein 40 g; Fat 35 g; Carbohydrate 5 g; Dietary Fibre 2 g; Cholesterol 155 mg; 2295 kJ (545 Cal)

Spiced liver curry

PREPARATION TIME: 25 MINUTES + 2 HOURS MARINATING | TOTAL COOKING TIME: 20 MINUTES | SERVES 4

60 ml (2 fl oz/¼ cup) dark soy sauce

3 garlic cloves, crushed

1 tablespoon sesame seeds, toasted

1 teaspoon sesame oil

500 g (1 lb/2 oz) chicken livers, trimmed
    and sliced

2 tablespoons olive oil

1 onion, sliced

1 red capsicum (pepper), sliced

1 teaspoon ground coriander

1 teaspoon ground cumin

2 tablespoons peanut oil

125 ml (4½ fl oz/½ cup) chicken stock

100 g (3½ oz) snow peas
    (mangetouts), trimmed

seasme seeds, toasted, to garnish

1   Combine the soy sauce, garlic, sesame seeds and sesame oil with 2 tablespoons water. Place the liver in a dish and pour over the marinade. Cover and refrigerate for 2 hours.

2   Heat half the olive oil in a large, heavy-based saucepan and cook the onion and capsicum over medium–low heat for 5–10 minutes, or until softened. Remove from the pan and set aside.

3   Sprinkle the liver with coriander and cumin and season well with pepper. Remove from the dish, reserving the marinade.

4   Heat the remaining olive oil and the peanut oil in a saucepan and add the liver. Cook over high heat, turning often, for about 3–5 minutes, or until firm but still slightly pink inside. Return the onion, capsicum and reserved marinade to the pan. Add the stock and snow peas, and simmer gently for 2–3 minutes. Serve immediately, with rice, if desired. Garnish with toasted sesame seeds.

NUTRITION PER SERVE
Protein 35 g; Fat 35 g; Carbohydrate 5 g; Dietary
Fibre 2 g; Cholesterol 705 mg; 2042 kJ (485 Cal)

Mix together the marinade ingredients and then pour over the liver to coat.

Add the chicken stock and snow peas, then simmer gently for 2-3 minutes.

Nasi goreng

PREPARATION TIME: 25 MINUTES | TOTAL COOKING TIME: 15 MINUTES | SERVES 4–6

5–8 long red chillies, seeded and chopped
2 teaspoons shrimp paste
8 garlic cloves, finely chopped
oil, for cooking
2 eggs, lightly beaten
350 g (12 oz) boneless, skinless chicken
    thighs, cut into thin strips
200 g (7 oz) peeled raw prawns (shrimps),
    deveined
1.5 kg (3 lb 5 oz/8 cups) cooked rice
80 ml (2½ fl oz/⅓ cup) kecap manis
80 ml (2½ fl oz/⅓ cup) soy sauce
2 small Lebanese (short) cucumbers, finely
    chopped
1 large tomato, finely chopped
lime wedges, to serve

1   Mix the chilli, shrimp paste and garlic in a food processor until the mixture resembles a paste.

2   Heat a wok until very hot, add 1 tablespoon of the oil and swirl it around to coat the side. Add the beaten egg and, using a metal spatula, push the egg up the edges of the wok to form a large omelette. Cook for 1 minute over medium heat, or until the egg is set, then flip it over and cook the other side for 1 minute. Remove from the wok and cool before slicing into strips.

3   Reheat the wok, add 1 tablespoon of the oil and stir-fry the chicken and half the chilli paste over high heat for about 4 minutes or until the chicken is just cooked. Remove the chicken from the wok.

4   Reheat the wok, add 1 tablespoon of the oil and stir-fry the prawns and the remaining chilli paste for about 3–4 minutes until the prawns are cooked. Remove the prawns from the wok and set aside.

5   Reheat the wok, add 1 tablespoon of the oil and the cooked rice, and toss constantly over medium heat for 4–5 minutes, or until the rice is heated through. Add the kecap manis and soy sauce, and toss constantly until all of the rice is coated in the sauces. Return the chicken and prawns to the wok, and toss until well combined and heated through. Season to taste with salt and pepper. Transfer to a large deep serving bowl and top with the omelette strips, cucumber and tomato. Serve with the lime wedges.

NUTRITION PER SERVE (6)
Protein 30 g; Fat 10 g; Carbohydrate 70 g; Dietary Fibre 3.5 g; Cholesterol 140 mg; 2105 kJ (505 Cal)

Slit the peeled prawns down the backs to remove the vein.

Process the chilli, shrimp paste and garlic until it forms a paste.

Chicken and peanut panang curry

PREPARATION TIME: 25 MINUTES I TOTAL COOKING TIME: 30–40 MINUTES I SERVES 4

1 tablespoon oil
1 large red onion, chopped
1–2 tablespoons panang curry paste
250 ml (9 fl oz/1 cup) coconut milk
500 g (1 lb/2 oz) boneless, skinless chicken
    thighs, cut into bite-sized pieces
4 makrut (kaffir lime) leaves
60 g (2¼ oz/¼ cup) coconut cream
1 tablespoon fish sauce
1 tablespoon lime juice
2 teaspoons soft brown sugar
80 g (2¾ oz/½ cup) roasted peanuts, chopped
1 handful Thai basil
80 g (2¾ oz/½ cup) chopped fresh pineapple
chilli sauce, to serve

1   Heat the oil in a wok or large frying pan.
Add the onion and curry paste to the wok and
stir over medium heat for 2 minutes. Add the
coconut milk and bring to the boil.

2   Add the chicken and makrut leaves to the
wok, then reduce the heat and cook for
15 minutes. Remove the chicken with a wire
mesh strainer or slotted spoon. Simmer the sauce
for 5 minutes, or until it is reduced and
quite thick.

3   Return the chicken to the wok. Add the
coconut cream, fish sauce, lime juice and brown
sugar. Cook for 5 minutes. Stir in the peanuts,
basil and pineapple. Serve with steamed rice.

Add the red onion and curry paste to the hot oil and
stir with a wooden spoon.

Stir in the chopped peanuts, basil and pineapple
just before serving.

NUTRITION PER SERVE
Protein 40 g; Fat 40 g; Carbohydrate 16 g; Dietary
Fibre 5 g; Cholesterol 63 mg; 2466 kJ (590 Cal)

Chiang Mai noodles

PREPARATION TIME: 20 MINUTES | TOTAL COOKING TIME: 15 MINUTES | SERVES 4

500 g (1 lb/2 oz) fresh egg noodles
1 tablespoon oil
3 red Asian or French shallots (eschalots),
    peeled and chopped
6 garlic cloves, chopped
2 teaspoons finely chopped red chilli, optional
1–2 tablespoons red curry paste
1 (350 g/12 oz) large boneless, skinless chicken
    breast, thinly sliced
1 carrot, cut into fine, thin strips
2 tablespoons fish sauce
2 teaspoons soft brown sugar
3 spring onions (scallions), thinly sliced
1 small handful coriander (cilantro) leaves

1 Cook the noodles in a wok or saucepan of rapidly boiling water for 2–3 minutes, or until they are just tender. Drain and keep warm.

2 Heat the oil in a wok or large frying pan until it is very hot. Add the shallots, garlic, chilli and curry paste, and stir-fry for 2 minutes, or until the mixture is fragrant. Add the chicken in two batches and cook for 3 minutes, or until the chicken changes colour.

3 Return all of the chicken to the wok. Add the carrot, fish sauce and brown sugar, and bring to the boil. Divide the noodles between serving bowls and mix in portions of the chicken mixture and spring onion. Top with the coriander leaves. Serve immediately.

HINT: *This dish must be served as soon as it is cooked or the noodles and vegetables will go soggy.*

Use a sharp knife to peel and finely chop the French shallots.

Place all the chicken back into the wok. Add the carrot, fish sauce and brown sugar.

NUTRITION PER SERVE
Protein 37 g; Fat 10 g; Carbohydrate 92 g; Dietary Fibre 4.5 g; Cholesterol 67 mg; 2565 kJ (612 Cal)

Vietnamese chicken curry

PREPARATION TIME: 30 MINUTES | TOTAL COOKING TIME: 1 HOUR | SERVES 4

1.5 kg (3 lb 5 oz) chicken pieces, such as
    thighs, drumsticks and wings
2 tablespoons oil
4 garlic cloves, finely chopped
5 cm (2 inch) piece fresh ginger, finely
    chopped
2 lemongrass stems, white part only,
    finely chopped
2 teaspoons dried chilli flakes
2 tablespoons Asian curry powder
    (see NOTE)
2 brown onions, chopped
2 teaspoons sugar
375 ml (13 fl oz/1½ cups) coconut milk
garlic chives, cut into long strips, to serve
coriander leaves (cilantro), to serve
roasted peanuts, to serve

1 Using a large heavy knife or cleaver, chop each piece of chicken into two, chopping straight through the bone. Pat the chicken pieces dry with paper towels.

2 Heat the oil in a large deep frying pan. Add the garlic, ginger, lemongrass, chilli and curry powder and stir constantly over medium heat for 3 minutes, or until fragrant. Add the chicken pieces, onion, sugar and 1 teaspoon of salt; toss gently. Cover, cook for 8 minutes, or until the onion has softened and then toss well to coat the chicken evenly with the curry mixture. Cover again and cook for 15 minutes over low heat—the chicken will gently braise, producing its own liquid.

3 Add the coconut milk and water to the pan. Bring to the boil, stirring occasionally. Reduce the heat and simmer, uncovered, for 30 minutes, or until the chicken is very tender. Serve garnished with the chives, coriander and peanuts.

NOTE: *Asian curry powders are available from speciality shops. There are different mixtures available for meat, chicken or fish.*

NUTRITION PER SERVE
Protein 60 g; Fat 26 g; Carbohydrate 11 g; Dietary Fibre 6 g; Cholesterol 125 mg; 2189 kJ (523 Cal)

Chop each piece of chicken into two pieces, or ask your butcher to do it.

Toss the chicken pieces through the curry mixture, using two wooden spoons.

Add the coconut milk and water to the curry and stir well.

Chicken and cashew stir-fry

PREPARATION TIME: 30 MINUTES I TOTAL COOKING TIME: 20 MINUTES I SERVES 4–6

oil, for cooking

750 g (1 lb 10 oz) boneless, skinless chicken
    thighs, cut into strips

2 egg whites, lightly beaten

60 g (2½ oz/½ cup) cornflour (cornstarch)

2 onions, thinly sliced

1 red capsicum (pepper), thinly sliced

200 g (7 oz) broccoli, cut into
    bite-sized pieces

2 tablespoons soy sauce

2 tablespoons dry sherry

1 tablespoon oyster sauce

50 g (1¾ oz/⅓ cup) roasted cashews

4 spring onions (scallions), diagonally sliced

1　Heat a wok until very hot, add 1 tablespoon
of the oil and swirl it around to coat the side.
Dip about a quarter of the chicken strips into the
egg white and then into the cornflour. Add to
the wok and stir-fry for 3–5 minutes, or until the
chicken is golden brown and just cooked. Drain
on paper towels and repeat with the remaining
chicken, reheating the wok and adding a little
more oil each time.

2　Reheat the wok, add 1 tablespoon of the oil
and stir-fry the onion, capsicum and broccoli
over medium heat for 4–5 minutes, or until the
vegetables have softened slightly. Increase the
heat to high and add the soy sauce, sherry and
oyster sauce. Toss the vegetables well in the sauce
and bring to the boil.

3　Return the chicken to the wok and toss over
high heat for 1–2 minutes to heat the chicken
and make sure it is entirely cooked through.
Season well with salt and freshly cracked pepper.
Toss the cashews and spring onion through the
chicken mixture, and serve immediately.

Dip the chicken strips into the egg white, then into
the cornflour.

Stir-fry the coated chicken in batches until it is
golden brown.

NUTRITION PER SERVE (6)
Protein 35 g; Fat 15 g; Carbohydrate 15 g; Dietary
Fibre 3 g; Cholesterol 60 mg; 1375 kJ (330 Cal)

Green chicken curry

PREPARATION TIME: 20 MINUTES I TOTAL COOKING TIME: 25 MINUTES I SERVES 4

1 tablespoon oil

1 onion, chopped

1–2 tablespoons green curry paste

375 ml (13 fl oz/1½ cups) coconut milk

500 g (1 lb 2 oz) boneless, skinless chicken
  thighs, cut into bite-sized pieces

100 g (3½ oz) green beans, cut into
  short pieces

6 makrut (kaffir lime) leaves

1 tablespoon fish sauce

1 tablespoon lime juice

1 teaspoon finely grated lime zest

2 teaspoons soft brown sugar

1 handful coriander (cilantro) leaves

1 Heat the oil in a wok or a heavy-based
frying pan. Add the onion and curry paste to
the wok and cook for about 1 minute, stirring
constantly. Add the coconut milk and 125 ml
(4 fl oz/½ cup) water and bring to the boil.

2 Add the chicken pieces, beans and makrut
leaves to the wok, and stir to combine. Simmer,
uncovered, for 15–20 minutes, or until the
chicken is tender. Add the fish sauce, lime juice,
lime zest and brown sugar to the wok, and stir
to combine. Sprinkle with fresh coriander leaves
just before serving. Serve with steamed rice.

NOTE: *Chicken thighs are sweet in flavour and a
very good texture for curries. You can use chicken
breasts instead, if you prefer. Do not overcook
them or they will be tough.*

NUTRITION PER SERVE
Protein 32 g; Fat 28 g; Carbohydrate 8 g; Dietary
Fibre 3 g; Cholesterol 63 mg; 1702 kJ (407 Cal)

Add the coconut milk and water to the wok and stir
with a wooden spoon.

After simmering, stir in the fish sauce, lime juice,
lime zest and brown sugar.

Indonesian spiced chicken

PREPARATION TIME: 15 MINUTES | TOTAL COOKING TIME: 1 HOUR | SERVES 6

1.5 kg (3 lb 5 oz) chicken thighs
1 large onion, roughly chopped
2 teaspoons crushed garlic
1 teaspoon grated fresh ginger
½ teaspoon ground turmeric
½ teaspoon ground pepper
2 teaspoons ground coriander
3 strips lemon zest or 3 makrut
   (kaffir lime) leaves
400 ml (14 fl oz) coconut milk
2 teaspoons soft brown or palm
   (jaggery) sugar

1 Wash the chicken under cold water, then pat dry with paper towels. Trim the chicken of excess fat. Place the onion, garlic and ginger in a food processor bowl or blender. Process until smooth, adding a little water if necessary. Place the chicken, onion mixture, turmeric, pepper, coriander, 1 teaspoon of salt, lemon zest or makrut, coconut milk, sugar and 250 ml (9 fl oz/1 cup) water in a saucepan and bring slowly to the boil.

2 Reduce the heat to a simmer. Cook, covered, for 45 minutes, or until the chicken is tender, stirring occasionally. Remove the chicken from the pan. Discard the lemon zest or makrut leaves.

3 Bring the sauce remaining in the pan to the boil. Reduce the heat to medium–high and cook, uncovered, stirring occasionally until thick. Place the chicken on a lightly oiled grill (broiler) and cook under high heat, browning the pieces on both sides. Serve the chicken with steamed rice and pour the sauce over the chicken. Sprinkle with freshly ground black pepper.

VARIATION: *The chicken pieces can be barbecued instead of grilled (broiled).*

NUTRITION PER SERVE
Protein 58 g; Fat 20 g; Carbohydrate 4.5 g; Dietary Fibre 1.5 g; Cholesterol 125 mg; 1778 kJ (425 Cal)

Place the chicken, onion mixture and the remaining ingredients in a saucepan.

Cook the chicken for 45 minutes, then remove from the saucepan.

Bring the sauce to the boil, then reduce the heat and cook, stirring occasionally, until thick.

Burmese chicken curry

PREPARATION TIME: 45 MINUTES | TOTAL COOKING TIME: 1 HOUR | SERVES 6

1 kg (2 lb/4 oz) chicken drumsticks or thighs
2 large onions, roughly chopped
3 large garlic cloves, peeled
5 cm (2 inch) piece fresh ginger, peeled
2 tablespoons peanut oil
½ teaspoon shrimp paste or 3 tablespoons
   fish sauce
500 ml (17 fl oz/2 cups) coconut milk
1 teaspoon chilli powder, optional

TRADITIONAL ACCOMPANIMENTS
200 g (7 oz) bean starch noodles
6 spring onions (scallions), diagonally sliced
4 tablespoons chopped coriander
   (cilantro) leaves
2 tablespoons garlic flakes, lightly fried
2 tablespoons onion flakes, lightly fried
3 lemons, cut into wedges
4 dried chillies, fried in oil to crisp
60 ml (2 fl oz/¼ cup) fish sauce

1   Pat the chicken with paper towels. Place the onion, garlic and ginger in a food processor, and process until smooth. Add a little water to help blend the mixture, if necessary.

2   Heat the oil in a pan and add the onion mixture. Add the shrimp paste and cook, stirring, over high heat for 5 minutes. Add the chicken and cook over medium heat, turning until browned. Add some salt, coconut milk and chilli powder and bring to the boil. Reduce the heat to a simmer and cook, covered, for 30 minutes, stirring occasionally. Uncover, cook for 15 minutes, or until the chicken is tender.

3   Meanwhile, place the noodles in a bowl and cover with boiling water. Set aside for 20 minutes. Drain, then place in a serving bowl. Place the traditional accompaniments in separate, small bowls. Each person helps themselves to a portion of noodles, chicken and a selection, or all, of the accompaniments.

Place the onion, garlic and ginger into a food processor and process until smooth.

Add 1 teaspoon of salt, coconut milk and chilli powder to the chicken mixture.

NUTRITION PER SERVE
Protein 33 g; Fat 27 g; Carbohydrate 15 g; Dietary Fibre 5 g; Cholesterol 62 mg; 1827 kJ (437 Cal)

Saffron chicken

PREPARATION TIME: 25 MINUTES | TOTAL COOKING TIME: 1 HOUR 20 MINUTES | SERVES 6

1 teaspoon saffron threads
2 tablespoons hot water
2 tablespoons oil
2 onions, chopped
3 garlic cloves crushed
3 cm (1¼ inch) piece fresh ginger, chopped
2 red chillies, seeded and sliced
1 teaspoon ground cardamom
1 teaspoon ground cumin
½ teaspoon ground turmeric
2 kg (4 lb 8 oz) chicken pieces (thighs, wings, drumsticks)
500 ml (17 fl oz/2 cups) chicken stock

1 Dry-fry the saffron threads in a frying pan over low heat for 1–2 minutes. Transfer to a small bowl, add the hot water and set aside.

2 Heat the oil in a saucepan over medium heat. Add the onion, garlic, ginger and chilli. Cover and cook for 10 minutes, or until very soft.

3 Add the cardamom, cumin and turmeric, and cook over medium heat for 2 minutes. Add the chicken pieces and cook over high heat for 3 minutes, or until the meat is well coated. Add the saffron liquid and the chicken stock. Bring to the boil, then reduce the heat and cook, covered, stirring occasionally, for 30 minutes.

4 Uncover, and cook for a further 20 minutes. Remove the chicken and keep warm. Reduce the stock to about 375 ml (13 fl oz/1½ cups) over very high heat. Pour over the chicken. Season to taste with salt and freshly ground black pepper. Serve with steamed rice.

Dry-fry the saffron threads in a frying pan over low heat for 1-2 minutes.

Remove the chicken from the saucepan and reduce the stock over high heat.

NUTRITION PER SERVE
Protein 45 g; Fat 15 g; Carbohydrate 3 g; Dietary Fibre 1 g; Cholesterol 155 mg; 1445 kJ (345 Cal)

Chicken and spinach curry

PREPARATION TIME: 25 MINUTES | TOTAL COOKING TIME: 1 HOUR 45 MINUTES | SERVES 4

2 tablespoons ghee (clarified butter)
1 kg (2 lb 4oz) chicken drumsticks and thighs
1 tablespoon hot curry powder
1 tablespoon curry paste
½ teaspoon black mustard seeds
½ teaspoon ground coriander
1 teaspoon paprika
¼ teaspoon cinnamon
½ teaspoon cumin
½ teaspoon turmeric
1 tablespoon finely chopped coriander root
2 garlic cloves, crushed
2 cm piece fresh ginger, grated
1 onion, chopped
1 kg (2 lb 4 oz) potatoes, quartered
375 ml (12 fl oz/1½ cups) chicken stock
1 tablespoon lemon juice
2 x 425 g (15 oz) tinned peeled
    whole tomatoes
250 g (9 oz) packet frozen spinach, defrosted
60 ml (2 fl oz/¼ cup) coconut cream

1 Melt 1 tablespoon of ghee in a heavy-based saucepan, and cook the chicken in batches for 2–3 minutes, or until browned all over. Remove. Melt the remaining ghee in the pan, add the curry powder, paste and remaining dry spices, and cook over low heat for 1–2 minutes, or until fragrant. Increase the heat, add the coriander root, garlic, ginger and onion, and cook for 3–5 minutes, or until the onion is soft.

2 Return the chicken pieces to the pan, add the potato and gently toss in the spices to coat. Season generously with salt and pepper. Pour in the chicken stock, and stir to ensure that any spices on the bottom of the pan are incorporated. Add the lemon juice and tomatoes, bring the mixture to the boil, then reduce the heat and simmer for 1–1½ hours, or until the potato is tender and the chicken meat is falling off the bones.

3 Carefully remove the chicken from the pan, let it cool slightly and pull the meat off the bones. Return to the pan. Stir in the spinach and coconut cream and cook for 3–5 minutes, or until heated through. Serve with rice.

NUTRITION PER SERVE
Protein 36 g; Fat 20 g; Carbohydrate 45 g; Dietary Fibre 12 g; Cholesterol 130 mg; 2115 kJ (505 Cal)

Melt the ghee, then cook the chicken in batches until browned all over.

Cook the curry powder, curry paste and dry spices until fragrant.

Gently toss the chicken and potatoes in the spices to coat.

Curried rice noodles with chicken

PREPARATION TIME: 25 MINUTES | TOTAL COOKING TIME: 10–15 MINUTES | SERVES 4–6

200 g (7 oz) thin rice stick noodles
1½ tablespoons oil
1 tablespoon red curry paste
3 boneless, skinless chicken thighs, cut into
   thin strips
1–2 teaspoons chopped red chilli
2 tablespoons fish sauce
2 tablespoons lime juice
100 g (3½ oz) bean sprouts
80 g (2¾ oz/½ cup) roasted chopped peanuts
2 tablespoons crisp-fried onion
2 tablespoons crisp-fried garlic
1 large handful coriander (cilantro) leaves

1   Cook the noodles in a saucepan of rapidly boiling water for 2 minutes. Drain and then toss with 2 teaspoons of the oil to prevent the strands from sticking together. Set aside.

2   Heat the remaining oil in a wok, add the curry paste and stir for 1 minute, or until fragrant. Add the chicken in batches and stir-fry for 2 minutes, or until golden brown. Return all of the chicken to the pan.

3   Add the chilli, fish sauce and lime juice. Bring to the boil and simmer for 1 minute. Add the bean sprouts and noodles and toss well. Arrange the noodles on a plate and sprinkle with the peanuts, onion, garlic and coriander leaves. Serve immediately.

Toss 2 teaspoons of oil through the noodles, using 2 wooden spoons.

Cook each batch of chicken for 2 minutes and return all of the chicken to the pan.

NUTRITION PER SERVE (6)
Protein 32 g; Fat 20 g; Carbohydrate 12 g; Dietary Fibre 3 g; Cholesterol 55 mg; 1452 kJ (345 Cal)

Fried crispy noodles (mee grob)

PREPARATION TIME: 30 MINUTES + 20 MINUTES DRYING | TOTAL COOKING TIME: 20 MINUTES | SERVES 4

100 g (3½ oz) rice vermicelli
500 ml (17 fl oz/2 cups) oil, for deep-frying
100 g (3½ oz) fried bean curd, cut into
    matchsticks
2 garlic cloves, finely chopped
4 cm (1½ inch) piece fresh ginger, grated
150 g (5½ oz) minced (ground) chicken
100 g (3½ oz) raw prawn (shrimp) meat,
    finely chopped
1 tablespoon white vinegar
2 tablespoons fish sauce
2 tablespoons soft brown sugar
2 tablespoons chilli sauce
1 teaspoon chopped red chilli
2 small knobs pickled garlic, chopped
1 handful garlic chives, snipped
1 large handful coriander (cilantro) leaves

1 Place the vermicelli in a bowl of hot water for 1 minute. Drain and allow to dry for 20 minutes. Heat the oil in a wok or deep frying pan, add the bean curd in two batches and cook for 1 minute, or until golden and crisp. Drain.

2 Add the completely dry vermicelli to the wok in several batches and cook for 10 seconds, or until puffed and crisp. Remove from the oil immediately to prevent the vermicelli absorbing too much oil. Drain on paper towels and allow to cool.

3 Drain all but 1 tablespoon of the oil from the wok. Reheat the wok over high heat and add the garlic, ginger, chicken and prawn meat; stir-fry for 2 minutes, or until golden brown. Add the vinegar, fish sauce, brown sugar, chilli sauce and chilli, and stir until boiling.

4 Just before serving, add the noodles and bean curd to the wok and toss thoroughly. Quickly toss through the pickled garlic, chives and coriander. Serve immediately.

NUTRITION PER SERVE
Protein 18 g; Fat 123 g; Carbohydrate 28 g; Dietary
Fibre 3 g; Cholesterol 56 mg; 5183 kJ (1238 Cal)

Cook the bean curd for 1 minute until golden brown. Remove with a wire mesh strainer.

Just before serving, return the noodles and bean curd to the wok, and toss thoroughly.

Ginger chicken with mushrooms and wheat noodles

PREPARATION TIME: 20 MINUTES + SOAKING | TOTAL COOKING TIME: 15 MINUTES | SERVES 4

4 dried Chinese mushrooms
2 teaspoons cornflour (cornstarch)
2 tablespoons soy sauce
2 tablespoons oyster sauce
1 tablespoon mirin or sweet sherry
200 g (7 oz) dried wheat noodles
1 teaspoon sesame oil
oil, for cooking
2–3 garlic cloves, crushed
8 cm (3 inch) piece fresh ginger, cut into
    matchsticks
375 g (13 oz) boneless, skinless chicken
    breasts, cut into thin strips
1 red onion, cut into thin wedges
6 spring onions (scallions), cut into
    short lengths
185 g (6½ oz) small field mushrooms,
    thickly sliced
90 g (3¼ oz/1 cup) bean sprouts
1 handul mint leaves

1 Soak the mushrooms in a small bowl of boiling water to soften them. Drain, then squeeze to remove the excess liquid. Remove the stems and thinkly slice the caps.

2 Combine the cornflour with 60 ml (2 fl oz/¼ cup) water and mix to a fine paste. Add the soy sauce, oyster sauce and mirin.

3 Cook the noodles in a large saucepan of boiling salted water for 1–2 minutes, or according to the manufacturer's instructions. Drain and set aside.

4 Heat the wok until very hot, add the sesame oil and 1 tablespoon of the oil, and swirl it around to coat the side. Stir-fry the garlic, ginger and chicken strips in batches over high heat for 2–3 minutes, or until the chicken is cooked through. Remove from the wok and set aside.

5 Reheat the wok, add 1 tablespoon of the oil and stir-fry the red onion and spring onion for 1–2 minutes, or until softened. Add the dried and field mushrooms, then stir-fry the mixture for 1–2 minutes, or until tender. Remove from the wok and set aside.

6 Add the soy sauce mixture to the wok and stir for 1–2 minutes, or until the sauce is well heated and slightly thickened. Return the chicken and vegetables to the wok with the bean sprouts, noodles and mint. Stir until the noodles are well coated with the sauce. Serve immediately.

NUTRITION PER SERVE
Protein 30 g; Fat 9 g; Carbohydrate 45 g; Dietary Fibre 6 g; Cholesterol 45 mg; 1650 kJ (395 Cal)

Cover the dried mushrooms with boiling water and leave to soak.

Cook the wheat noodles in a large saucepan of boiling salted water.

Honey chicken

PREPARATION TIME: 15 MINUTES | TOTAL COOKING TIME: 25 MINUTES | SERVES 4

oil, for cooking
500 g (1 lb/2 oz) boneless, skinless chicken
    thighs, cut into cubes
1 egg white, lightly beaten
40 g (1½ oz/⅓ cup) cornflour (cornstarch)
2 onions, thinly sliced
1 green capsicum (pepper), cubed
2 carrots, cut into matchsticks
100 g (3½ oz) snow peas (mangetouts), sliced
90 g (3¼ oz/¼ cup) honey
2 tablespoons toasted almonds

1   Heat a wok until very hot, gradually add
1½ tablespoons of the oil and swirl it around to
coat the side. Dip half of the chicken into the
egg white, then lightly dust with the cornflour.
Stir-fry over high heat for 4–5 minutes, or until
the chicken is golden brown and just cooked.
Remove from the wok and drain on paper
towels. Repeat with the remaining chicken, then
remove all the chicken from the wok.

2   Reheat the wok, add 1 tablespoon of the oil
and stir-fry the sliced onion over high heat for
3–4 minutes, or until slightly softened. Add the
capsicum and carrot, and cook, tossing, for
3–4 minutes, or until tender. Stir in the snow
peas and cook for 2 minutes.

3   Increase the heat, add the honey and toss the
vegetables until well coated. Return the chicken
to the wok and toss until it is heated through
and is well coated in the honey. Remove from
the heat and season to taste with salt and pepper.
Serve immediately, sprinkled with the almonds.

Dip the chicken into the egg white, then lightly dust
with the cornflour.

Stir-fry the chicken pieces until golden brown and
just cooked.

NUTRITION PER SERVE
Protein 35 g; Fat 20 g; Carbohydrate 35 g; Dietary
Fibre 4 g; Cholesterol 60 mg; 1815 kJ (435 Cal)

Crisp-skinned chicken

PREPARATION TIME: 1 HOUR + COOLING | TOTAL COOKING TIME: 25 MINUTES | SERVES 4

1.3 kg (3 lb) whole chicken
1 tablespoon honey
1 star anise
1 strip dried mandarin zest (see NOTE)
oil, for deep-frying
2 lemons, cut into wedges

FIVE-SPICE SALT

2 tablespoons sea salt
1 teaspoon white peppercorns
½ teaspoon Chinese five-spice
½ teaspoon ground white pepper

1 Place the chicken in a saucepan and cover with cold water. Add the honey, star anise, mandarin zest and 1 teaspoon of salt, and bring to the boil. Reduce the heat and simmer for 15 minutes. Turn off the heat and leave the chicken, covered, for 15 minutes. Transfer the chicken to a plate, and cool. Cut the chicken in half lengthways. Place on paper towels, uncovered, in the refrigerator for 20 minutes.

2 Heat the oil in a wok or deep, heavy-based pan. It is hot enough to use when a piece of bread dropped into the oil turns brown in 30 seconds. Very gently lower in half the chicken, skin-side down. Cook for 6 minutes, then turn and cook for another 6 minutes, making sure all the skin comes in contact with the oil. Drain on paper towels. Repeat with the remaining chicken.

3 To make the five-spice salt, put the sea salt and peppercorns in a frying pan and dry-fry until fragrant and the salt is slightly browned. Crush in a mortar and pestle. Mix with the five-spice and white pepper. Joint the chicken and serve sprinkled with the five-spice salt and with lemon wedges.

NOTE: *To make dried mandarin peel, preheat the oven to 180°C (350°F/Gas 4). Remove all of the pith from strips of peel and bake for 15 minutes.*

NUTRITION PER SERVE
Protein 45 g; Fat 15 g; Carbohydrate 7 g; Dietary Fibre 1.5 g; Cholesterol 100 mg; 1482 kJ (355 Cal)

Use poultry scissors to cut the cooled chicken in half lengthways.

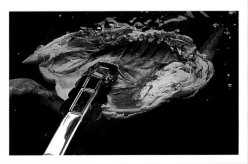
Gently lower half the chicken, skin side down, into the oil.

Chicken chow mein

PREPARATION TIME: 25 MINUTES + 1 HOUR MARINATING | TOTAL COOKING TIME: 25 MINUTES | SERVES 4–6

500 g (1 lb/2 oz) boneless, skinless chicken
    thighs, cut into small cubes
1 tablespoon cornflour (cornstarch)
2 tablespoons soy sauce
1 tablespoon oyster sauce
2 teaspoons sugar
3 tablepoons vegetable oil, for cooking
2 onions, thinly sliced
2 garlic cloves, finely chopped
1 tablespoon finely chopped fresh ginger
1 green capsicum (pepper), cubed
2 celery stalks, diagonally sliced
8 spring onions (scallions), cut into
    short pieces
100 g (3½ oz) mushrooms, thinly sliced
80 g (2¾ oz/½ cup) water chestnuts,
    thinly sliced
2 teaspoons cornflour, extra
1 tablespoon dry sherry
125 ml (4 fl oz/½ cup) chicken stock
1 tablespoon soy sauce, extra
90 g (3¼ oz) Chinese cabbage,
    finely shredded
200 g (7 oz) ready-prepared fried noodles

1 In a glass or ceramic bowl, combine the chicken with the cornflour, soy sauce, oyster sauce and sugar. Cover and refrigerate for 1 hour.

2 Heat the wok until very hot, gradually add 1 tablespoon of the oil and swirl it around to coat the side. Stir-fry the chicken in two batches over high heat for 4–5 minutes, or until cooked. Add oil between batches. Remove all the chicken from the wok and set it aside.

3 Reheat the wok, add 1 tablespoon of the oil and stir-fry the onion over medium–high heat for 3–4 minutes, or until the onion is slightly softened. Add the garlic, ginger, capsicum, celery, spring onion, mushrooms and water chestnuts to the wok. Stir-fry over high heat for 3–4 minutes, or until tender.

4 Combine the extra cornflour with the sherry, chicken stock and soy sauce. Add to the wok and bring to the boil. Simmer for 1–2 minutes, or until the sauce thickens slightly. Stir in the cabbage and cook, covered, for 1–2 minutes, or until the cabbage is just wilted. Return the chicken to the wok and toss until heated through. Season to taste with salt and freshly ground pepper. Arrange the noodles around the edge of a large platter and spoon the chicken mixture into the centre. Serve immediately.

Combine the cornflour, sherry, stock and soy sauce, and pour into the wok.

NUTRITION PER SERVE (6)
Protein 25 g; Fat 8.5 g; Carbohydrate 20 g; Dietary Fibre 4 g; Cholesterol 55 mg; 1110 kJ (265 Cal)

Noodles with chicken and fresh black beans

PREPARATION TIME: 15 MINUTES I TOTAL COOKING TIME: 15 MINUTES I SERVES 2–3

2 teaspoons salted black beans
oil, for cooking
2 teaspoons sesame oil
500 g (1 lb 2 oz) boneless. skinless chicken
    thighs, cut into thin strips
3 garlic cloves, very thinly sliced
4 spring onions (scallions), chopped
1 teaspoon sugar
1 red capsicum (pepper), sliced
100 g (3½ oz) green beans, cut into
    short pieces
300 g (10½ oz) Hokkien noodles
2 tablespoons oyster sauce
1 tablespoon soy sauce

1 Rinse the black beans in running water. Drain and roughly chop.

2 Heat a wok until very hot, add 1 tablespoon of oil and the sesame oil and swirl it around to coat the side. Stir-fry the chicken in three batches, until well browned, tossing regularly. Remove from the wok and set aside.

3 Reheat the wok, add 1 tablespoon of the oil and stir-fry the garlic and spring onion for about 1 minute. Add the black beans, sugar, capsicum and green beans, and cook for 1 minute. Sprinkle with 2 tablespoons of water, cover and steam for 2 minutes.

4 Gently separate the noodles and add to the wok with the chicken, oyster sauce and soy sauce, and toss well to combine. Cook, covered, for about 2 minutes, or until the noodles are just softened.

Cut the chicken thighs into thin strips, removing any excess fat.

Roughly chop the rinsed and drained black beans with a sharp knife.

NUTRITION PER SERVE (3)
Protein 50 g; Fat 20 g; Carbohydrate 50 g; Dietary
Fibre 2 g; Cholesterol 85 mg; 2490 kJ (595 Cal)

Ginger chicken with black fungus

PREPARATION TIME: 25 MINUTES | TOTAL COOKING TIME: 15 MINUTES | SERVES 4

15 g (½ oz/¼ cup) black (wood) fungus
   (see NOTE)
1 tablespoon oil
3 garlic cloves, chopped
6 cm (2½ inch) piece fresh ginger, cut into
   thin shreds
500 g (1 lb 2 oz) boneless, skinless chicken
   breast, sliced
4 spring onions (scallions), chopped
1 tablespoon soy sauce
1 tablespoon fish sauce
2 teaspoons brown sugar
½ red capsicum (pepper), thinly sliced
1 handful coriander (cilantro) leaves
4 tablespoons Thai basil

1   Soak the fungus in a bowl of hot water for 15 minutes, or until soft and swollen, then drain and chop roughly.

2   Heat the oil in a large wok, add the garlic and ginger and stir-fry for 1 minute. Add the chicken and stir-fry in batches over high heat for 2–3 minutes or until the chicken changes colour. Return all of the chicken to the wok. Add the spring onion and soy sauce, and stir-fry for 1 minute.

3   Add the fish sauce, brown sugar and fungus to the pan. Stir thoroughly, then cover and steam for 2 minutes. Serve immediately, scattered with the capsicum, coriander and basil.

NOTE: *Black (wood) fungus is a dried mushroom that swells to many times its size when soaked in hot water. Available from Chinese supermarkets and good greengrocers.*

When the fungus is soft and swollen, drain it well and chop it with a sharp knife.

Cover the wok and allow the mixture to steam for 2 minutes.

NUTRITION PER SERVE
Protein 30 g; Fat 8 g; Carbohydrate 3.5 g; Dietary Fibre 1 g; Cholesterol 62 mg; 842 kJ (200 Cal)

Chicken and apple curry

PREPARATION TIME: 20 MINUTES | TOTAL COOKING TIME: 1 HOUR 5 MINUTES | SERVES 4–6

1 kg (2 lb 4 oz) chicken wings
60 ml (2 fl oz/¼ cup) oil
1 large onion, sliced
1 tablespoon curry powder
1 large carrot, chopped
1 celery stalk, sliced
400 ml (14 fl oz) coconut cream
250 ml (9 fl oz/1 cup) chicken stock
2 green apples, chopped
30 g (1 oz/¼ cup) sultanas (golden raisins)
80 g (2¾ oz/½ cup) roasted peanuts, optional

NUTRITION PER SERVE (6)
Protein 27 g; Fat 37 g; Carbohydrate 20 g; Dietary
Fibre 5 g; Cholesterol 42 mg; 2133 kJ (510 Cal)

1 Pat the chicken wings dry with paper towels. Tuck the wing tips to the underside.

2 Heat 2 tablespoons of the oil in a large heavy-based saucepan and add the chicken in small batches. Cook quickly over medium heat for 5 minutes, or until well browned on both sides. Drain on paper towels.

3 Heat the remaining oil in the pan. Add the onion and curry powder and cook, stirring, over medium heat for 3 minutes, or until soft.

4 Return the chicken to the pan. Add the carrot, celery, coconut cream and stock, and bring to the boil. Reduce the heat and simmer. Cook, covered, for 30 minutes. Add the apple, coriander and sultanas, and cook for a further 20 minutes, or until the chicken is cooked, stirring occasionally. Sprinkle with roasted peanuts, if you wish.

VARIATIONS: *Pear may be used instead of apple in this recipe. Curry paste may be used instead of curry powder.*

Pat the chicken wings dry, then tuck the tips of the wings to the underside.

Cook the chicken in small batches over medium heat until well browned.

Cook the onion and curry powder, stirring, for 3 minutes, or until soft.

Thai potato and chicken curry

PREPARATION TIME: 20 MINUTES I TOTAL COOKING TIME: 30 MINUTES I SERVES 4–6

250 g (9 oz) boneless, skinless chicken thighs
250 g (9 oz) orange sweet potato, peeled
300 g (10½ oz) potatoes, peeled
2 tablespoons oil
1 onion, chopped
1–2 tablespoons Thai yellow curry paste
¼ teaspoon ground turmeric
410 ml (14½ fl oz/1⅔ cups) coconut milk
2 makrut (kaffir lime) leaves
2 teaspoons fish sauce
2 teaspoons soft brown sugar
1 tablespoon lime juice
1 teaspoon lime zest
50 g (1¾ oz/⅓ cup) roasted peanuts, roughly
   chopped

1 Remove the excess fat from the chicken and cut into bite-sized pieces. Cut the sweet potato and potatoes into bite-sized pieces. Heat the oil in a large heavy-based saucepan or wok and cook the onion until softened. Add the curry paste and turmeric and stir for 1 minute, or until aromatic.

2 Stir in the coconut milk and 250 ml (9 fl oz/1 cup) of water and bring to the boil. Reduce the heat and add the potato, sweet potato, chicken and makrut leaves. Simmer for 15–20 minutes, or until the vegetables are tender and the chicken is cooked through.

3 Add the fish sauce, sugar, lime juice and lime zest and stir to combine. Garnish with the peanuts and serve with rice.

NOTE: *Thai yellow curry paste is not as common as the red or green but is available from most Asian food stores.*

Peel the orange sweet potato and chop into bite-sized pieces.

When the onion has softened, stir in the curry paste and turmeric.

NUTRITION PER SERVE (6)
Protein 10 g; Fat 35 g; Carbohydrate 15 g; Dietary
Fibre 3 g; Cholesterol 40 mg; 1805 kJ (430 Cal)

Lemon chilli chicken

PREPARATION TIME: 20 MINUTES | TOTAL COOKING TIME: 35 MINUTES | SERVES 4

2 garlic cloves, chopped
1 tablespoon grated fresh ginger
2 tablespoons olive oil
600 g (1 lb 5 oz) boneless, skinless
    chicken thighs
1 teaspoon ground coriander
2 teaspoons ground cumin
½ teaspoon ground turmeric
1 red chilli, chopped
125 ml (4 fl oz/½ cup) lemon juice
185 ml (6 fl oz/¾ cup) white wine
1 handful coriander (cilantro) leaves, to serve

1 Blend the garlic, ginger and 1 tablespoon water into a paste in a small food processor or mortar and pestle. Heat the olive oil in a heavy-based saucepan and brown the chicken in batches. Remove with a slotted spoon and set aside.

2 Add the garlic paste to the pan and cook, stirring, for 1 minute. Add the coriander, cumin, turmeric and chilli and stir-fry for 1 minute more. Stir in the lemon juice and wine.

3 Add the chicken pieces to the pan and stir to combine. Bring to the boil, then reduce the heat, cover and cook, stirring, for 20–25 minutes, or until the chicken is tender. Remove the lid and cook the sauce over high heat for 5 minutes to reduce it by half. Season to taste with salt and pepper. Serve on a bed of steamed jasmine rice and sprinkle with coriander leaves.

NUTRITION PER SERVE
Protein 30 g; Fat 15 g; Carbohydrate 0 g; Dietary Fibre 0 g; Cholesterol 105 mg; 1290 kJ (310 Cal)

Brown the chicken in batches to stop the meat from stewing.

Add the coriander, cumin, turmeric and chilli and stir-fry for 1 minute.

Pasta

Chicken and pumpkin cannelloni

PREPARATION TIME: 1 HOUR | TOTAL COOKING TIME: 1 HOUR 15 MINUTES | SERVES 6

500 g (1 lb 2 oz) butternut pumpkin

3 tablespoons olive oil

100 g (3½ oz) pancetta, roughly chopped

2 garlic cloves, crushed

500 g (1 lb 2 oz) minced (ground) chicken

½ teaspoon garam masala

2 tablespoons chopped flat-leaf (Italian) parsley

150 g (5½ oz) goat's cheese

50 g (1¾ oz) ricotta cheese

375 g (13 oz) instant cannelloni tubes

100 g (3½ oz/1 cup) grated parmesan cheese

TOMATO SAUCE

30 g (1 oz) butter

1 garlic clove, crushed

2 x 425 g (15 oz) tinned chopped tomatoes

3 tablespoons chopped flat-leaf (Italian) parsley

60 ml (2 fl oz/¼ cup) white wine

1 Preheat the oven to 220°C (425°F/ Gas 7). Brush the pumpkin with 1 tablespoon of the olive oil and bake on a baking tray for 40 minutes, or until tender. Scrape out the flesh of the cooked pumpkin and mash with a fork. Set aside to cool.

2 Add 1 tablespoon of the oil to a heavy-based frying pan and cook the pancetta over medium heat for 2–3 minutes. Remove from the pan and drain on paper towels.

3 In the same pan heat the remaining oil. Add the garlic and stir for 30 seconds. Add the chicken in small batches and brown, making sure the chicken is cooked through. Remove from the pan and drain on paper towels. Reduce the oven to 200°C (400°F/Gas 6).

4 Combine the pumpkin with the pancetta and chicken. Mix in the garam marsala, parsley, goat's cheese and ricotta. Season. Fill a cannelloni tube with the chicken mixture. Repeat with the rest of the tubes and filling.

5 To make the tomato sauce, melt the butter in a heavy-based saucepan and add the garlic. Cook for 1 minute, then add the tomato and simmer over medium heat for 1 minute. Add the parsley and white wine, and simmer for another 5 minutes. Season with salt and freshly ground pepper, to taste.

6 Arrange the cannelloni tubes over a little of the tomato sauce on the bottom of a 3 litre (12 cups) capacity ovenproof dish. Spoon the remaining tomato sauce over the cannelloni and sprinkle with the parmesan. Bake for about 20–25 minutes, or until the cheese is golden.

NUTRITION PER SERVE
Protein 44 g; Fat 26 g; Carbohydrate 55 g; Dietary Fibre 6.5 g; Cholesterol 113 mg; 2670 kJ (638 cal)

Scrape out the flesh of the cooked pumpkin and mash with a fork.

Combine the pumpkin, pancetta, chicken and other filling ingredients in a bowl.

Arrange the cannelloni tubes over a little of the tomato sauce in the dish.

Spaghetti with chicken meatballs

PREPARATION TIME: 30 MINUTES + CHILLING | TOTAL COOKING TIME: 1 HOUR 30 MINUTES | SERVES 4–6

500 g (1 lb 2 oz) minced (ground) chicken
60 g (2¼ oz) grated parmesan cheese
160 g (5½ oz/2 cups) fresh white breadcrumbs
2 garlic cloves, crushed
1 egg
1 tablespoon chopped flat-leaf (Italian) parsley
1 tablespoon chopped sage
60 ml (2 fl oz/¼ cup) oil
500 g (1 lb 2 oz) spaghetti
2 tablespoons chopped oregano, to serve

TOMATO SAUCE
1 tablespoon olive oil
1 onion, finely chopped
2 kg (4 lb 8 oz) tomatoes, roughly chopped
2 bay leaves
1 large handful basil
1 teaspoon coarse ground black pepper

1   In a large bowl, mix together the chicken, parmesan, breadcrumbs, garlic, egg, parsley, sage and some freshly ground black pepper. Shape tablespoons of the mixture into small balls and chill for 30 minutes to firm. Heat the oil in a shallow frying pan and fry the balls in batches until golden brown, turning often by shaking the pan. Drain on paper towels.

2   To make the tomato sauce, heat the oil in a large saucepan, add the onion and fry for 1–2 minutes. Add the tomato and bay leaves, cover and bring to the boil, stirring occasionally. Reduce the heat to low, partially cover and cook for 50–60 minutes.

3   Add the meatballs, basil and pepper, and simmer, uncovered, for 10–15 minutes. Cook the spaghetti in boiling water until *al dente*. Drain, then return to the pan. Add some sauce to the pasta and toss gently to combine. Serve the pasta in individual bowls with the remaining sauce and the meatballs, sprinkled with fresh oregano.

Shape tablespoons of the chicken mixture into small balls.

Add the meatballs, basil and pepper to the tomato mixture.

NUTRITION PER SERVE (6)
Protein 40 g; Fat 20 g; Carbohydrate 83 g; Dietary Fibre 9.5 g; Cholesterol 80 mg; 2890 kJ (690 cal)

Chicken agnolotti with buttered sage sauce

PREPARATION TIME: 15 MINUTES | TOTAL COOKING TIME: 15 MINUTES | SERVES 4

500 g (1 lb 2 oz) fresh or dried chicken-filled
   agnolotti or ravioli
60 g (2 ¼ oz/¼ cup) butter
4 spring onions (scallions), chopped
2 tablespoons chopped sage
3 tablespoons grated parmesan cheese, to serve
sage leaves, chopped, to serve

1   Add the pasta to a large saucepan of rapidly
boiling water and cook until *al dente*. Drain the
pasta, then return to the pan.

2   While the pasta is cooking, melt the butter in
a heavy-based frying pan. Add the spring onion
and sage, and stir for 2 minutes. Season with salt
and ground black pepper.

3   Add the sauce to the pasta and toss well.
Pour onto a warmed serving platter and sprinkle
with the parmesan and sage. Serve immediately.

HINT: *Bite through a piece of pasta to test
whether it is done.*

NUTRITION PER SERVE
Protein 16 g; Fat 24 g; Carbohydrate 18 g; Dietary
Fibre 2 g; Cholesterol 74 mg; 1445 kJ (345 Cal)

Add the spring onion and sage to the melted butter,
and stir for 2 minutes.

Chicken ravioli

PREPARATION TIME: 45 MINUTES + 30 MINUTES STANDING | TOTAL COOKING TIME: 1 HOUR | SERVES 4

PASTA
250 g (9 oz/2 cups) plain (all-purpose) flour
3 eggs
1 tablespoon olive oil
1 egg yolk, extra

FILLING
125 g (4½ oz) minced (ground) chicken
75 g (2½ oz) ricotta or cottage cheese
2 tablespoons grated parmesan cheese
60 g (2¼ oz) chicken livers, trimmed and
    chopped
30 g (1 oz) prosciutto, chopped
1 slice salami, chopped
1 egg, beaten
1 tablespoon chopped parsley
1 garlic clove, crushed
¼ teaspoon mixed spice

TOMATO SAUCE
2 tablespoons olive oil
1 onion, finely chopped
2 garlic cloves, crushed
2 x 425 g (15 oz) tinned chopped tomatoes
1 handful chopped basil
½ teaspoon mixed herbs

1 To make the pasta, sift the flour and a pinch of salt onto a board. Make a well in the centre of the flour. In a bowl, whisk together the eggs, oil and 1 tablespoon water. Add the egg mixture gradually to the flour, working in with your hands until the mixture forms a ball. Knead on a lightly floured surface for about 5 minutes, or until smooth and elastic. Place the dough in a lightly oiled bowl and cover with plastic wrap. Allow to stand for 30 minutes.

2 To make the filling, place the chicken, both cheeses, liver, prosciutto, salami, egg, parsley, garlic and mixed spice in a food processor. Process until finely chopped. Season to taste with salt and freshly ground black pepper.

3 To make the tomato sauce, heat the oil in a medium saucepan. Add the onion and garlic and stir over low heat until the onion is tender. Increase the heat, add the undrained tomatoes, basil, mixed herbs and season with salt and pepper. Stir to combine, then bring to the boil. Reduce the heat and simmer for 15 minutes. Remove from the heat.

4 Roll out half the pasta dough until 2 mm (1/16 inch) thick. Cut with a knife or fluted pastry cutter into 10 cm (4 inch) strips. Place teaspoons of the filling at 5 cm (2 inch) intervals down one side of each strip.

5 Whisk together the extra egg yolk and 3 tablespoons water. Brush along one side of the dough and between the filling. Fold the dough over the filling to meet the other side. Repeat with the remaining filling and dough. Press the edges of the dough firmly together to seal. Cut between the mounds of filling with a knife or a fluted pastry cutter.

6 Cook the ravioli in batches in a large saucepan of rapidly boiling water for 10 minutes each batch. Reheat the tomato sauce in a saucepan. Serve the sauce with the ravioli.

NUTRITION PER SERVE
Protein 30 g; Fat 25 g; Carbohydrate 60 g; Dietary Fibre 6 g; Cholesterol 223 mg; 2534 kJ (605 Cal)

Knead the pasta mixture on a lightly floured surface until smooth and elastic.

Place the filling ingredients in a food processor and process until finely chopped.

Place teaspoons of the filling at 5 cm (2 inch) intervals down one side of each strip.

Chicken ravioli with fresh tomato sauce

PREPARATION TIME: 40 MINUTES I TOTAL COOKING TIME: 40 MINUTES I SERVES 4

TOMATO SAUCE

1 tablespoon oil
1 large onion, chopped
2 garlic cloves, crushed
90 g (3¼ oz/⅓ cup) tomato paste
    (concentrated purée)
60 ml (2 fl oz/¼ cup) red wine
170 ml (5½ fl oz/⅔ cup) chicken stock
2 tomatoes, chopped
1 tablespoon chopped basil

RAVIOLI

200 g (7 oz) minced (ground) chicken
1 tablespoon chopped basil
3 tablespoons grated parmesan cheese
3 spring onions (scallions), finely chopped
50 g (1¾ oz) ricotta cheese
250 g (9 oz) packet (48) round won ton
    or gow gee wrappers

1 To make the tomato sauce, heat the oil in a saucepan and add the onion and garlic. Cook for 2–3 minutes, then stir in the tomato paste, wine, stock and tomato, and simmer for 20 minutes. Stir in the basil, and season with salt and freshly ground black pepper.

2 To make the ravioli, combine the chicken, basil, parmesan, spring onion, ricotta and some salt and pepper. Lay half of the wrappers on a flat surface and brush with a little water. Place slightly heaped teaspoons of the mixture onto the centre of each wrapper. Place another wrapper on top and press the edges firmly together to seal.

3 Bring a large saucepan of water to the boil. Add the ravioli, a few at a time, and cook for 2–3 minutes, or until just tender. Drain well and serve with the tomato sauce.

For the ravioli, combine the chicken, basil, parmesan, spring onion and ricotta.

Place the mixture between two wrappers and press together to make the ravioli.

NUTRITION PER SERVE
Protein 24 g; Fat 5.5 g; Carbohydrate 50 g; Dietary Fibre 6 g; Cholesterol 37 mg; 1520 kJ (363 Cal)

Fettuccine with chicken and mushroom sauce

PREPARATION TIME: 10 MINUTES | TOTAL COOKING TIME: 25 MINUTES | SERVES 4

2 boneless, skinless chicken breasts
1 tablespoon olive oil
30 g (1 oz) butter
2 bacon slices, cut into thin strips
2 garlic cloves, crushed
250 g (9 oz) button mushrooms, sliced
80 ml (2½ fl oz/⅓ cup) dry white wine
170 ml (5½ fl oz/⅔ cup) cream
4 spring onions (scallions), chopped
1 tablespoon plain (all-purpose) flour
400 g (14 oz) fettuccine
4 tablespoons shaved parmesan cheese

1 Trim the chicken of excess fat and sinew, and cut into strips. Heat the oil and butter in a heavy-based frying pan. Add the chicken and cook over medium heat for 3 minutes, or until browned.

2 Add the bacon, garlic and mushrooms, and cook over medium-high heat for 2 minutes, stirring occasionally.

3 Add the wine and cook until the liquid has reduced by half. Add the cream and spring onion, and bring to the boil. Blend the flour with 2 tablespoons water until smooth. Add to the pan and stir over the heat until the mixture boils and thickens, then reduce the heat and simmer for 2 minutes. Season to taste and keep warm.

4 Cook the fettuccine in a large saucepan of rapidly boiling water until *al dente*. Pour the sauce over the fettuccine and sprinkle with parmesan cheese. Serve immediately with herb bread on the side.

NUTRITION PER SERVE
Protein 40 g; Fat 35 g; Carbohydrate 75 g; Dietary Fibre 7 g; Cholesterol 136 mg; 3380 kJ (808 Cal)

Add the bacon, garlic and mushrooms to the chicken and cook over medium heat.

Add the cream and spring onion to the pan and bring to the boil.

Chicken tortellini with tomato sauce

PREPARATION TIME: 30 MINUTES + RESTING | TOTAL COOKING TIME: 30 MINUTES | SERVES 4

PASTA
250 g (9 oz/2 cups) plain (all-purpose) flour
3 eggs
1 tablespoon olive oil

FILLING
20 g (¾ oz) butter
80 g (2¾ oz) chicken breast, cubed
2 slices pancetta, chopped
50 g (1¾ oz/½ cup) grated parmesan cheese
½ teaspoon nutmeg
1 egg, lightly beaten

TOMATO SAUCE
80 ml (2½ fl oz/⅓ cup) olive oil
1.5 kg (3 lb 5 oz) fresh ripe tomatoes, peeled
   and chopped
3 tablespoons chopped oregano
50 g (1¾ oz/½ cup) grated parmesan cheese
100 g (3½ oz) fresh bocconcini, thinly sliced,
   to serve

1 To make the pasta, sift the flour and a pinch of salt and make a well in the centre. Whisk together the eggs, oil and 1 tablespoon water. Add the egg mixture gradually to the flour, mixing to a firm dough. Gather together into a ball, adding a little extra water if necessary. Knead on a floured surface for 5 minutes, or until the dough is smooth. Place in a lightly oiled bowl and cover. Leave for 30 minutes.

2 To make the filling, heat the butter in a frying pan, add the chicken and cook until golden brown, then drain. Process the chicken and pancetta in a food processor until finely chopped. Transer to a bowl and add the parmesan, nutmeg, egg and salt and freshly ground pepper, to taste.

3 Roll out the dough very thinly on a lightly floured surface. Using a floured cutter, cut into 5 cm (2 inch) rounds. Spoon about ½ teaspoon of filling into the centre of each round. Fold the rounds in half to form semi-circles, pressing the edges together firmly. Wrap each semi-circle around your finger to form a ring and then press the ends of the dough together firmly.

4 To make the tomato sauce, put the oil, tomato and oregano in a frying pan and cook over medium-high heat for 10 minutes. Stir in the parmesan.

5 Cook the tortellini in two batches in rapidly boiling water for about 6 minutes each batch, or until *al dente*. Drain well and return to the pan. Reheat the tomato sauce. Divide the tortellini among bowls, top with tomato sauce and bocconcini and allow the cheese to melt a little before serving.

NUTRITION PER SERVE
Protein 33 g; Fat 44 g; Carbohydrate 53 g; Dietary Fibre 7 g; Cholesterol 230 mg; 3090 kJ (740 Cal)

Place the dough in a lightly oiled bowl, cover with plastic wrap and leave.

Roll out the dough very thinly on a lightly floured surface. Cut into rounds with a floured pastry cutter.

Wrap the semi-circles around your finger to make a ring and press the ends together.

Stir-fried chicken and pasta

PREPARATION TIME: 20 MINUTES I TOTAL COOKING TIME: 15 MINUTES I SERVES 4–6

270 g (9 ½ oz) jar sun-dried (sun-blushed)
   tomatoes in oil
3 chicken breasts, cut into thin strips
2 garlic cloves, crushed
125 ml (4 fl oz/½ cup) cream
2 tablespoons shredded basil
400 g (14 oz) penne pasta, cooked
2 tablespoons pine nuts, toasted

1 Drain the sun-dried tomatoes, reserving the oil. Thinly slice the sun-dried tomatoes.

2 Heat a wok until very hot, add 1 tablespoon of the reserved oil and swirl it around to coat the side. Stir-fry the chicken strips in batches, adding more oil when necessary.

3 Return all the chicken strips to the wok and add the garlic, sun-dried tomatoes and cream. Simmer gently for 4–5 minutes.

4 Divide the pasta among serving bowls, top with the sauce and sprinkle with the basil and toasted pine nuts.

NUTRITION PER SERVE (6)
Protein 30 g; Fat 30 g; Carbohydrate 5 g; Dietary
Fibre 4 g; Cholesterol 70 mg; 2696 kJ (640 Cal)

Toast the pine nuts by dry-frying them in a hot wok, stirring regularly.

Drain the sun-dried tomatoes, reserving the oil, and thinly slice them.

Return the chicken to the wok with the garlic, sun-dried tomatoes and cream.

Conchiglie with chicken and ricotta

PREPARATION TIME: 15 MINUTES | TOTAL COOKING TIME: 1 HOUR 10 MINUTES | SERVES 4

500 g (1 lb 2 oz) conchiglie (shell pasta)
2 tablespoons olive oil
1 onion, chopped
1 garlic clove, crushed
60 g (2¼ oz) prosciutto, sliced
125 g (4½ oz) mushrooms, chopped
250 g (9 oz) minced (ground) chicken
2 tablespoons tomato paste
    (concentrated purée)
425 g (15 oz) tinned chopped tomatoes
125 ml (4 fl oz/½ cup) dry white wine
1 teaspoon dried oregano
250 g (9 oz) ricotta cheese
150 g (5½ oz/1 cup) grated mozzarella cheese
1 teaspoon snipped chives
1 tablespoon chopped flat-leaf
    (Italian) parsley
3 tablespoons grated parmesan cheese

1 Add the conchiglie to a large saucepan of rapidly boiling water and cook until *al dente*. Drain well. Heat the oil in a large frying pan. Add the onion and garlic and stir over low heat until the onion is tender. Add the prosciutto and stir for 1 minute.

2 Add the mushrooms to the pan and cook for 2 minutes. Add the chicken and brown well, breaking up any lumps with a fork as it cooks.

3 Stir in the tomato paste, undrained tomatoes, wine, oregano, salt and pepper. Bring to the boil, then reduce the heat and simmer for 20 minutes.

4 Preheat the oven to 180°C (350°F/Gas 4). Combine the ricotta, mozzarella, chives, parsley and half the parmesan. Spoon a little of the mixture into each pasta shell. Spoon some of the chicken sauce into the base of a casserole dish. Arrange the conchiglie on top. Spread the remaining sauce over the top. Sprinkle with the remaining parmesan and bake for 25–30 minutes, or until golden.

NUTRITION PER SERVE
Protein 40 g; Fat 28 g; Carbohydrate 91 g; Dietary
Fibre 8 g; Cholesterol 70 mg; 3339 kJ (800 Cal)

Brown the chicken mince well, breaking up with a fork as it cooks.

Spoon a little of the cheese mixture into each pasta shell.

Chicken and vegetable lasagne

PREPARATION TIME: 45 MINUTES | TOTAL COOKING TIME: 1 HOUR 20 MINUTES | SERVES 8

500 g (1 lb 2 oz) boneless, skinless
    chicken breasts
cooking oil spray
2 garlic cloves, crushed
1 onion, chopped
2 zucchini (courgettes), chopped
2 celery stalks, chopped
2 carrots, chopped
300 g (10½ oz) pumpkin, diced
2 x 400 g (14 oz) tinned chopped tomatoes
2 thyme sprigs
2 bay leaves
125 ml (4 fl oz/½ cup) white wine
2 tablespoons tomato paste
    (concentrated purée)
2 tablespoons chopped basil
500 g (1 lb 2 oz) English spinach
500 g (1 lb 2 oz) reduced-fat cottage cheese
450 g (1 lb) ricotta cheese
60 ml (2 fl oz/¼ cup) skim milk
½ teaspoon ground nutmeg
300 g (10½ oz) instant or fresh lasagne sheets
3 tablespoons grated parmesan cheese

1 Preheat the oven to 180°C (350°F/Gas 4). Trim excess fat from the chicken breasts, then finely mince in a food processor. Heat a large, deep, non-stick frying pan, spray lightly with oil and cook the chicken in batches until browned. Remove and set aside.

2 Add the garlic and onion to the pan and cook until softened. Return the chicken to the pan and add the zucchini, celery, carrot, pumpkin, tomato, thyme, bay leaves, wine and tomato paste. Simmer, covered, for 20 minutes. Remove the bay leaves and thyme, stir in the basil and set aside.

3 Shred the spinach and set aside. Mix the cottage and ricotta cheeses, skim milk, nutmeg and half the parmesan.

4 Spoon a little of the tomato mixture over the base of a large casserole dish and top with a single layer of lasagne sheets. Top with half the remaining tomato mixture, then the spinach and spoon over half the cheese mixture. Continue with another layer of lasagne sheets, the remaining tomato and another layer of lasagne sheets. Spread the remaining cheese mixture on top and sprinkle with parmesan. Bake for 40–50 minutes, or until golden. The top may puff up slightly but will settle on standing.

NUTRITION PER SERVE
Protein 40 g; Fat 10 g; Carbohydrate 35 g; Dietary Fibre 7 g; Cholesterol 70 mg; 1790 kJ (430 Cal)

Finely mince the trimmed chicken breasts in a food processor.

Add the vegetables with the thyme, bay leaves, wine and tomato paste to the pan.

Tagliatelle with chicken livers and cream

PREPARATION TIME: 20 MINUTES | TOTAL COOKING TIME: 15 MINUTES | SERVES 4

1 onion
300 g (10½ oz) chicken livers
2 tablespoons olive oil
1 garlic clove, crushed
250 ml (9 fl oz/1 cup) cream
1 tablespoon snipped chives
1 teaspoon wholegrain mustard
2 eggs, beaten
375 g (13 oz) tagliatelle pasta
2 tablespoons shaved parmesan cheese,
    to serve
snipped chives, extra to serve

1 Chop the onion finely. Trim the chicken livers and chop them into small pieces.

2 Heat the oil in a large frying pan. Add the onion and garlic and stir over low heat until the onion is tender. Add the chicken livers to the pan. Cook gently for 2–3 minutes. Remove from the heat and stir in the cream, chives, mustard and salt and pepper, to taste. Return to the heat and bring to the boil. Add the egg and stir quickly to combine. Remove from the heat.

3 While the sauce is cooking, add the tagliatelle to a large saucepan of rapidly boiling water and cook until *al dente*. Drain well and return to the pan. Add the sauce to the hot pasta and toss well to combine. Serve in warmed pasta bowls and sprinkle with the parmesan cheese and chives.

HINT: *Snip the chives with kitchen scissors.*

Trim all of the chicken livers, then cut them into small pieces.

Add the beaten egg to the sauce mixture, and stir quickly to combine.

NUTRITION PER SERVE
Protein 34 g; Fat 38 g; Carbohydrate 69 g; Dietary Fibre 4 g; Cholesterol 217 mg; 3175 kJ (760 Cal)

Spaghetti with chicken bolognaise

PREPARATION TIME: 10 MINUTES | TOTAL COOKING TIME: 15 MINUTES | SERVES 4

2 tablespoons olive oil
2 leeks, trimmed, thinly sliced
1 red capsicum (pepper), finely chopped
2 garlic cloves, crushed
500 g (1 lb 2 oz) minced (ground) chicken
500 g (1 lb 2 oz/2 cups) tomato passata
    (puréed tomatoes)
1 tablespoon chopped thyme
1 tablespoon chopped rosemary
2 tablespoons pitted and chopped
    black olives
400 g (14 oz) spaghetti pasta
125 g (4½ oz) feta cheese, crumbled
Thyme sprigs, to serve

1 Heat the oil in a large, heavy-based frying pan. Add the leek, capsicum and garlic and cook over medium–high heat for 2 minutes, or until lightly browned.

2 Add the chicken and cook over high heat for 3 minutes, or until browned and any liquid has evaporated. Stir occasionally to break up any lumps as the chicken cooks.

3 Add the tomato passata, thyme and rosemary, and bring to the boil. Reduce the heat and simmer, uncovered, for 5 minutes, or until the sauce has reduced and thickened. Add the olives and stir to combine. Season with salt and freshly ground pepper.

4 Meanwhile, cook the spaghetti in a large saucepan of rapidly boiling water until *al dente*; drain. Place the spaghetti on individual serving plates or pile into a large deep serving dish and pour the chicken mixture over the top. Sprinkle with the feta and thyme and serve immediately.

VARIATION: *Any type of pasta, dried or fresh, is suitable to use. Freshly grated parmesan or pecorino cheese can be used instead of feta.*

NUTRITION PER SERVE
Protein 50 g; Fat 23 g; Carbohydrate 88 g; Dietary Fibre 10 g; Cholesterol 84 mg; 3158 kJ (758 Cal)

Remove the seeds and white membrane from the capsicum and finely chop the flesh.

Add the chicken mince to the leek, capsicum and garlic in the pan.

Grills and pan-fries

Barbecued garlic chicken

PREPARATION TIME: 20 MINUTES + MARINATING | TOTAL COOKING TIME: 10 MINUTES | SERVES 4

6 garlic cloves, crushed
1½ tablespoons cracked black peppercorns
1 handful chopped coriander (cilantro) leaves
   and stems
4 coriander (cilantro) roots, chopped
80 ml (2½ fl oz/⅓ cup) lime juice
1 teaspoon soft brown sugar
1 teaspoon ground turmeric
2 teaspoons light soy sauce
4 boneless, skinless chicken breasts

CUCUMBER AND TOMATO SALAD
1 Lebanese (short) cucumber, unpeeled
1 large roma (plum) tomato
¼ small red onion, thinly sliced
1 small red chilli, finely chopped
2 tablespoons coriander (cilantro) leaves
2 tablespoons lime juice
1 teaspoon soft brown sugar
1 tablespoon fish sauce

1 Blend the garlic, peppercorns, coriander, lime juice, sugar, turmeric and soy sauce in a food processor until smooth then transfer the marinade to a bowl.

2 Remove the tenderloins from the chicken breasts. Score the top of each breast three times. Add the breasts and tenderloins to the marinade, cover and refrigerate for 2 hours or overnight, turning the chicken occasionally.

3 To make the salad, halve the cucumber and scoop out the seeds with a teaspoon. Cut into slices. Halve the tomato lengthways and slice crossways. Combine the cucumber, tomato, onion, chilli and coriander in a small bowl. Drizzle with the combined lime juice, sugar and fish sauce.

4 Cook the chicken on a lightly greased barbecue grill or flat plate for 3 minutes on each side, or until cooked through and tender. Serve the chicken immediately with the salad.

NUTRITION PER SERVE
Protein 52 g; Fat 5.5 g; Carbohydrate 6 g; Dietary Fibre 2 g; Cholesterol 110 mg; 1195 kJ (285 Cal)

Separate the tenderloins from the chicken breasts by pulling them away.

Use a teaspoon to scoop the seeds out of the halved cucumber.

Drizzle the combined lime juice, sugar and fish sauce over the salad ingredients.

Chicken burger with tangy garlic mayonnaise

PREPARATION TIME: 20 MINUTES + 3 HOURS MARINATING I TOTAL COOKING TIME: 15 MINUTES I SERVES 4

4 boneless, skinless chicken breasts
125 ml (4 fl oz/½ cup) lime juice
1 tablespoon sweet chilli sauce
4 bacon slices
4 hamburger buns, halved
4 lettuce leaves
1 large tomato, sliced

GARLIC MAYONNAISE
2 egg yolks
2 garlic cloves, crushed
1 tablespoon dijon mustard
1 tablespoon lemon juice
125 ml (4 fl oz/½ cup) olive oil

1   Place the chicken in a shallow non-metallic dish. Prick the chicken breasts with a skewer several times. Combine the lime juice and sweet chilli sauce in a bowl. Pour the mixture over the chicken, cover and refrigerate for several hours or overnight.

2   To make the mayonnaise, place the egg yolks, garlic, mustard and lemon juice in a food processor bowl or blender and process until smooth. With the motor running, add the oil in a thin, steady stream. Process until the mixture reaches a thick consistency. Refrigerate, covered, until required.

3   Preheat a barbecue grill or flatplate to high. Remove and discard the rind from the bacon, and cut the bacon in half crossways. Lightly grease the hot barbecue. Cook the chicken and bacon for 5 minutes, or until crisp. Cook the chicken for a further 5–10 minutes, or until well browned and cooked through, turning once.

4   Toast the hamburger buns until lightly browned. Arrange the lettuce, tomato, chicken and bacon on the bases. Top with the garlic mayonnaise and finish with the remaining bun top.

Pour the combined lime juice and sweet chilli sauce over the chicken fillets.

Add the oil to the egg yolk mixture in a thin steady stream.

NUTRITION PER SERVE
Protein 70 g; Fat 42 g; Carbohydrate 52 g; Dietary Fibre 5 g; Cholesterol 211 mg; 3624 kJ (866 Cal)

Thai chicken cutlets

PREPARATION TIME: 20 MINUTES + 1 HOUR MARINATING | TOTAL COOKING TIME: 20 MINUTES | SERVES 4–6

12 boneless, skinless chicken thighs
   (1.25 kg/2 lb 12 oz)
6 garlic cloves
1 teaspoon black peppercorns
3 coriander (cilantro) roots and stems, roughly
   chopped

CHILLI GARLIC DIP
4–5 dried red chillies
2 large garlic cloves, chopped
60 g (2¼ oz) sugar
80 ml (2½ fl oz/⅓ cup) dry cider or rice
   vinegar
60 ml (2 fl oz/¼ cup) boiling water

1 Trim the chicken thighs of any excess fat and sinew. Place the garlic, peppercorns, coriander and a pinch of salt salt in a food processor. Process for 20–30 seconds, or until the mixture forms a smooth paste. (This can also be done using a mortar and pestle.) Place the chicken in a shallow non-metallic dish. Spread the garlic mixture over the chicken. Refrigerate the chicken, covered, for 1 hour.

2 To make the chilli garlic dip, soak the chillies in hot water for 20 minutes. Drain the chillies and chop finely. Place in a mortar with the garlic and sugar, and grind to a smooth paste. Place the mixture in a small saucepan and add the vinegar, a pinch of salt and boiling water. Bring to the boil, then reduce the heat and simmer for 2–3 minutes. Set aside to cool.

3 Preheat a barbecue grill or flat plate to high. Grease the barbecue and cook the chicken for 5–10 minutes on each side, or until cooked through, turning once. Serve with the chilli garlic dip.

Place the garlic, peppercorns, coriander and salt in a food processor bowl.

Cook the chicken on a greased barbecue grill or flat plate.

NUTRITION PER SERVE (6)
Protein 47 g; Fat 5 g; Carbohydrate 0.5 g; Dietary Fibre 1 g; Cholesterol 105 mg; 1005 kJ (240 Cal)

Buffalo wings with ranch dressing

PREPARATION TIME: 25 MINUTES + 3 HOURS MARINATING | TOTAL COOKING TIME: 25 MINUTES | SERVES 4

8 large chicken wings
2 teaspoons black pepper
2 teaspoons garlic salt
2 teaspoons onion powder
olive oil, for deep-frying
125 ml (4 fl oz/½ cup) tomato
    sauce (ketchup)
2 tablespoons worcestershire sauce
20 g (¾ oz) butter, melted
2 teaspoons sugar
Tabasco sauce, to taste

RANCH DRESSING
125 g (4½ oz/½ cup) whole-egg mayonnaise
125 g (4½ oz/½ cup) sour cream
2 tablespoons lemon juice
2 tablespoons snipped chives

NUTRITION PER SERVE
Protein 44 g; Fat 40 g; Carbohydrate 18 g; Dietary
Fibre 1 g; Cholesterol 157 mg; 2539 kJ (605 Cal)

1   Pat the chicken wings dry with paper towels. Cut the tips off each wing and discard. Bend each wing back to snap the joint, and cut through to create two pieces. Combine the pepper, garlic salt and onion powder. Rub into each chicken piece.

2   Heat the oil to moderately hot in a deep heavy-based frying pan. Cook the chicken in batches for 2 minutes. Remove and drain on paper towels.

3   Transfer the chicken to a non-metallic bowl or shallow dish. Combine the sauces, butter, sugar and Tabasco. Pour the mixture over the chicken and stir to coat. Refrigerate, covered, for several hours or overnight.

4   To make the ranch dressing, combine the mayonnaise, sour cream, lemon juice, chives, salt and white pepper in a bowl and mix well.

5   Preheat a barbecue grill or flat plate to high. Lightly oil the hot barbecue. Cook the chicken for 5 minutes, turning and brushing with the marinade. Serve with the dressing.

Bend the wings back to snap the joint, then cut through to make two pieces.

Cook the chicken in batches in the hot oil, then remove and drain on paper towels.

Pour the sauce mixture over the chicken and stir to coat.

Chargrilled chicken

PREPARATION TIME: 20 MINUTES + 2 HOURS MARINATING | TOTAL COOKING TIME: 1 HOUR | SERVES 4

4 boneless, skinless chicken breasts
2 tablespoons honey
1 tablespoon wholegrain mustard
1 tablespoon soy sauce
2 red onions, cut into wedges
8 roma (plum) tomatoes, halved lengthways
2 tablespoons soft brown sugar
2 tablespoons balsamic vinegar
cooking oil spray
1 tablespoon basil, for serving

1 Preheat the oven to 180°C (350°F/Gas 4). Trim the chicken of any excess fat and place in a shallow dish. Combine the honey, mustard and soy sauce and pour over the chicken, tossing to coat evenly. Cover and refrigerate for 2 hours, turning once.

2 Place the onion wedges and tomato halves on a baking tray covered with baking paper. Sprinkle with the sugar and drizzle with the balsamic vinegar. Bake for 40 minutes.

3 Heat a chargrill pan and lightly spray with oil. Remove the chicken from the marinade and cook for 4–5 minutes on each side, or until cooked through. Slice the chicken and serve with the tomato halves, onion wedges and basil.

Drizzle the balsamic vinegar over the onion wedges and tomato halves.

Cook the marinated chicken in a hot, lightly oiled chargrill pan.

NUTRITION PER SERVE
Protein 25 g; Fat 2.5 g; Carbohydrate 30 g; Dietary Fibre 3 g; Cholesterol 50 mg; 990 kJ (235 Cal)

Smoked chicken breast

PREPARATION TIME: 5 MINUTES I TOTAL COOKING TIME: 25 MINUTES I SERVES 4

4 boneless, skinless chicken breasts
1 tablespoon olive oil
seasoned pepper, to taste
hickory or mesquite chips, for smoking

1   Prepare a kettle barbecue for indirect cooking at medium heat. Trim the chicken of excess fat and sinew. Brush the chicken with the oil and sprinkle with the seasoned pepper.

2   Spoon a pile of hickory or mesquite chips (about 25) over the coals in each charcoal rail.

3   Cover the barbecue and cook the chicken for 15 minutes. Test with a sharp knife. If the juices do not run clear, cook for another 5–10 minutes, or until cooked through. Serve with chilli noodles.

NUTRITION PER SERVE
Protein 50 g; Fat 10 g; Carbohydrate 0 g; Dietary Fibre 0 g; Cholesterol 116 mg; 1208 kJ (288 Cal)

Brush the chicken breasts with the oil and sprinkle with the seasoned pepper.

Spoon some hickory or mesquite chips over the coals in each charcoal rail.

Test the chicken with a sharp knife to check that the juices run clear.

Chicken breast with fruit medley

PREPARATION TIME: 25 MINUTES + 3 HOURS MARINATING | TOTAL COOKING TIME: 20 MINUTES | SERVES 4

4 boneless, skinless chicken breasts
80 ml (2½ fl oz/⅓ cup) white wine
60 ml (2 fl oz/¼ cup) olive oil
2 teaspoons grated fresh ginger
1 garlic clove, crushed

FRUIT MEDLEY
225 g (8 oz) tinned pineapple slices, drained
1 small mango
2 small kiwi fruit
150 g (5½ oz) watermelon, seeds removed
1 tablespoon finely chopped mint leaves

1   Trim the chicken breasts of fat and sinew. Place the chicken in a shallow non-metallic dish. Combine the wine, oil, ginger and garlic in a bowl, and pour over the chicken. Refrigerate, covered, for several hours or overnight, turning occasionally.

2   To make the fruit medley, finely chop the pineapple, mango, kiwi fruit and watermelon. Combine with the mint and refrigerate.

3   Preheat a barbecue grill or flat plate to high. Lightly oil the hot barbecue. Cook the marinated chicken for 5–10 minutes each side, or until well browned on the outside and cooked through. Serve immediately with the fruit medley.

NUTRITION PER SERVE
Protein 50 g; Fat 20 g; Carbohydrate 15 g; Dietary Fibre 3 g; Cholesterol 110 mg; 2000 kJ (480 Cal)

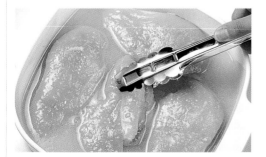

Marinate the chicken in the wine, oil, ginger and garlic mixture, turning occasionally.

Cook the chicken on a hot barbecue grill until well browned on the outside.

For the fruit medley, finely chop the pineapple, mango, kiwi fruit and watermelon.

Citrus chicken drumsticks

PREPARATION TIME: 20 MINUTES + 3 HOURS MARINATING | TOTAL COOKING TIME: 20 MINUTES | SERVES 4

8 chicken drumsticks
80 ml (2½ fl oz/⅓ cup) orange juice
80 ml (2½ fl oz/⅓ cup) lemon juice
1 teaspoon grated orange zest
1 teaspoon grated lemon zest
1 teaspoon sesame oil
1 tablespoon olive oil
1 spring onion (scallion), finely chopped

1   Pat the chicken drumsticks dry with paper towels. Trim any excess fat and score the thickest part of the chicken with a knife. Place in a shallow non-metallic dish.

2   Combine the juices, zests, oils and spring onion. Pour over the chicken. Refrigerate, covered, for several hours or overnight, turning occasionally.

3   Preheat a barbecue grill or flat plate to high. Drain the chicken, reserving the marinade. Lightly grease the hot barbecue grill or flat plate. Cook the drumsticks for 15–20 minutes, or until tender. Brush occasionally with the reserved marinade. Serve immediately.

NUTRITION PER SERVE
Protein 43 g; Fat 10 g; Carbohydrate 3.5 g; Dietary Fibre 0 g; Cholesterol 94 mg; 1175 kJ (280 Cal)

Score the thickest part of the chicken drumsticks with a knife.

Remove the chicken from the marinade, reserving the marinade.

Cook the drumsticks until tender, brushing with the reserved marinade.

Chicken fajitas

PREPARATION TIME: 35 MINUTES + 3 HOURS MARINATING | TOTAL COOKING TIME: 20 MINUTES | SERVES 4

4 boneless, skinless chicken breasts
2 tablespoons olive oil
60 ml (2 fl oz/¼ cup) lime juice
2 garlic cloves, crushed
1 teaspoon ground cumin
2 tablespoons chopped coriander
    (cilantro) leaves
8 flour tortillas
1 tablespoon olive oil, extra
2 onions, sliced
2 green capsicums (peppers), cut into
    thin strips
125 g (4½ oz/1 cup) grated cheddar cheese
1 large avocado, sliced
250 g (9 oz/1 cup) bottled tomato salsa

1 Trim the chicken of fat and sinew, and cut into thin strips. Place the chicken strips in a shallow non-metallic dish. Combine the oil, lime juice, garlic, cumin and coriander in a jug, and mix well. Pour the mixture over the chicken. Cover with plastic wrap, refrigerate for several hours or overnight.

2 Preheat a barbecue grill or flat plate to high. Wrap the tortillas in foil and place on a cool part of the barbecue grill to warm through for 10 minutes. Heat the oil on a flat plate. Cook the onion and capsicum for 5 minutes, or until soft. Move the vegetables to a cooler part of the plate to keep warm.

3 Place the chicken and marinade on the flat plate and cook for 5 minutes, or until cooked through. Transfer the chicken, vegetables and wrapped tortillas to a serving platter. Make up individual fajitas by placing the chicken, onion and capsicum, cheese and avocado over the tortillas. Top with the salsa and roll up to enclose the filling.

NUTRITION PER SERVE
Protein 88 g; Fat 59 g; Carbohydrate 116 g; Dietary Fibre 9.5 g; Cholesterol 173 mg; 5660 KJ (1352 Cal)

Combine the oil, lime juice, garlic, cumin and coriander, and pour over the chicken.

Cook the onion and capsicum on the flat plate until soft.

Chicken cutlets with corn relish

PREPARATION TIME: 20 MINUTES | TOTAL COOKING TIME: 25 MINUTES | SERVES 4

8 chicken thigh cutlets, skin on
    (1 kg/2 lb 4 oz)
1 tablespoon olive oil
1 small clove garlic, crushed
¼ teaspoon ground turmeric

CORN RELISH
200 g (7 oz/1⅓ cups) frozen corn kernels
1 tablespoon olive oil
1 red chilli, seeded and chopped
1 small green capsicum (pepper), finely
    chopped
1 onion, finely chopped
80 ml (2½ fl oz/⅓ cup) white vinegar
60 g (2¼ oz) sugar
1 teaspoon wholegrain mustard
3 teaspoons cornflour (cornstarch)
1 teaspoon sweet paprika
1 teaspoon finely chopped coriander
    (cilantro) leaves, extra, whole leaves
    to serve
1 tablespoon olive oil, extra

NUTRITION PER SERVE
Protein 47 g; Fat 20 g; Carbohydrate 30 g; Dietary
Fibre 2 g; Cholesterol 100 mg; 2047 kJ (490 Cal)

1   Preheat a barbecue grill or flat plate to high. Trim the chicken of excess fat and sinew. Prick the skin of the chicken cutlets with the point of a knife. Place the cutlets in a large frying pan of boiling water. Reduce the heat and simmer for 5 minutes. Remove from the pan, then drain and allow to cool.

2   Place the olive oil, garlic, turmeric and salt in a bowl and whisk to combine. Rub the mixture over the skin side of the chicken cutlets. Set aside.

3   To make the corn relish, cook the corn in a saucepan of boiling water for 2–3 minutes, or until tender, then drain. Heat the oil in a saucepan. Add the chilli, capsicum and onion. Cook over medium heat until tender. Add the corn, vinegar, sugar and mustard, and cook, stirring, for a further 5 minutes. Mix the cornflour with 125 ml (4 fl oz/½ cup) water. Pour into the corn mixture. Bring to the boil, then reduce the heat and stir until thickened. Stir in the paprika, coriander and extra oil. Remove from the heat and cool.

4   Lightly grease the hot barbecue grill or flat plate. Cook the cutlets, skin side up for 2 minutes, then turn and cook for 4 minutes. Continue cooking for another 5–10 minutes, turning frequently, until the chicken is well browned and cooked through. Serve with the corn relish and sprinkle with coriander leaves.

Simmer the chicken cutlets in a large frying pan of boiling water.

Pour the blended cornflour and water into the corn mixture.

Cook the chicken cutlets, turning frequently, until the chicken is well browned and cooked through.

Kettle chicken

PREPARATION TIME: **10** MINUTES | TOTAL COOKING TIME: **1** HOUR | SERVES 4–6

1.8 kg (4 lb) chicken
1 bulb garlic
1 large handful oregano
60 ml (2 fl oz/¼ cup) olive oil

1 Prepare a kettle barbecue for indirect cooking at medium heat. Place a drip tray underneath the top grill.

2 Remove the giblets and any large fat deposits from the chicken. Wipe the chicken and pat dry with paper towels. Season the chicken cavity with salt and cracked black pepper. Using a sharp knife, cut the top off the bulb of garlic. Push the whole bulb of garlic, unpeeled, into the cavity, then add the whole handful of oregano. Close the cavity with several toothpicks or a skewer.

3 Rub the chicken skin with salt and brush with olive oil. To barbecue the chicken, tie the legs together and tuck the wing tips under. Place the chicken on the barbecue over the drip tray. Put the lid on the barbecue and cook for 1 hour, brushing occasionally with the olive oil to keep the skin moist. Insert a skewer into the chicken thigh. If the juices run clear, the chicken is cooked through. Stand the chicken away from the heat for 5 minutes before carving.

4 Carefully separate the garlic cloves and serve 1 or 2 cloves with each serving of chicken. (The flesh can be squeezed from the clove and eaten with the chicken.)

Cut the top off the bulb of garlic, then push the whole bulb of garlic into the cavity.

Insert a skewer into the thickest part of the chicken thigh to see if the chicken is cooked.

NUTRITION PER SERVE
Protein 42 g; Fat 16 g; Carbohydrate 0.5 g; Dietary Fibre 1 g; Cholesterol 138 mg; 1328 kJ (317 Cal)

Honey-glazed chicken breasts

PREPARATION TIME: 10 MINUTES + 20 MINUTES MARINATING | TOTAL COOKING TIME: 10 MINUTES | SERVES 6

Double the honey & bbq sauce

6 boneless, skinless chicken breasts
50 g (1¾ oz) butter, softened
90 g (3¼ oz/¼ cup) honey
60 ml (2 fl oz/¼ cup) barbecue sauce
2 teaspoons wholegrain mustard

1   Trim the chicken of any excess fat and sinew. Using a sharp knife, make three or four diagonal cuts across one side of each chicken breast. Preheat a barbecue grill or flatplate to high.

2   Combine the butter, honey, barbecue sauce and mustard in a small bowl. Spread half of the honey mixture thickly over the slashed side of the chicken. Cover with plastic wrap and stand at room temperature for 20 minutes. Set the remaining honey mixture aside.

3   Lightly grease the hot barbecue grill or flatplate. Cook the chicken breasts, slashed side up first, for 2–3 minutes each side, or until the chicken is cooked through and tender. Brush with the reserved honey mixture several times during cooking. Serve with a mixed salad.

HINT: *Any leftover cooked chicken can be shredded and served mixed through a green salad or sliced thickly and made into sandwiches.*

NOTES: *Barbecue the chicken just before serving. The chicken can be marinated overnight in the refrigerator. When honey is cooked, its sugars caramelise and some of its flavour is lost. For a distinctive taste to this dish, use a dark honey with a strong flavour, such as leatherwood, lavender or rosemary. Lighter honeys, such as yellow box, orange blossom or clover, will sweeten and glaze the meat without necessarily affecting its flavour. Usually the paler the honey, the milder its flavour.*

Use a sharp knife to make three or four diagonal cuts on one side of the chicken.

Combine the butter, honey, barbecue sauce and mustard in a small bowl.

NUTRITION PER SERVE
Protein 38 g; Fat 11 g; Carbohydrate 16 g; Dietary Fibre 0 g; Cholesterol 105 mg; 1297 kJ (310 Cal)

Chicken burger with tarragon mayonnaise

PREPARATION TIME: 25 MINUTES | TOTAL COOKING TIME: 15 MINUTES | SERVES 6

1 kg (2 lb 4 oz) minced (ground) chicken
1 small onion, finely chopped
2 teaspoons lemon zest
2 tablespoons sour cream
80 g (2¾ oz/1 cup) fresh breadcrumbs
6 onion bread rolls
1 handful rocket (arugula) leaves,
   to serve
3 tomatoes, cut into wedges, to serve

TARRAGON MAYONNAISE

1 egg yolk
1 tablespoon tarragon vinegar
½ teaspoon dijon mustard
250 ml (9 fl oz/1 cup) olive oil

1   Place the chicken in a mixing bowl. Add the onion, lemon zest, sour cream and breadcrumbs. Using your hands, mix until thoroughly combined. Divide the mixture into 6 equal portions and shape into 1.5 cm (⅝ inch) thick patties.

2   Preheat a barbecue grill or flat plate to high. Lightly oil the hot barbecue. Cook the patties for 7 minutes each side, turning once. Serve the patties on the onion rolls with the mayonnaise.

3   To make the tarragon mayonnaise, place the egg yolk, half the vinegar and the mustard in a small mixing bowl. Whisk together for about 1 minute, or until light and creamy. Add the oil about 1 teaspoon at a time, whisking constantly until the mixture thickens. Increase the flow of oil to a thin stream and continue whisking until all of the oil has been incorporated. Stir in the remaining vinegar and season to taste.

4   Put the patties on the rolls with rocket and mayonnaise. Serve with some tomato wedges on the side and sprinkle with freshly ground black pepper.

NUTRITION PER SERVE
Protein 40 g; Fat 47 g; Carbohydrate 11 g; Dietary Fibre 1 g; Cholesterol 122 mg; 2628 kJ (628 Cal)

HINT: *The mayonnaise can also be made in a food processor. Add the oil in a thin stream, with the motor constantly running, until the mixture thickens and turns creamy.*

Mix the chicken mince, onion, lemon zest, sour cream and breadcrumbs together.

Cook the patties for 7 minutes each side, turning once, or until they are cooked through.

Once the mayonnaise mixture has thickened, add the oil in a steady stream.

Tandoori barbecue chicken

PREPARATION TIME: 15 MINUTES + 4 HOURS MARINATING | TOTAL COOKING TIME: 1 HOUR | SERVES 4

4 chicken leg quarters (marylands), skin removed
1 teaspoon salt
2 garlic cloves, crushed
1 tablespoon lemon juice
250 g (9 oz/1 cup) plain yoghurt
1½ teaspoons garam masala
½ teaspoon ground black pepper
½ teaspoon ground turmeric
2–3 drops red food colouring
20–30 mesquite or hickory chips, for smoking
olive oil, for basting

1 Place the chicken in a large non-metallic dish and rub with the salt and garlic. Combine the lemon juice, yoghurt, garam masala, pepper and turmeric in a bowl. Add enough food colouring to make the marinade a bright orange–red colour. Pour the marinade over the chicken and coat evenly with the back of a spoon. Refrigerate, covered, for 4 hours, turning the chicken every hour.

2 Prepare a kettle barbecue for indirect cooking. When the barbecue coals are covered with fine white ash, add the mesquite or hickory chips to the coals. Cover the barbecue and leave until the smoke is well established (about 5 minutes).

3 Brush the barbecue grill with oil. Arrange the chicken on the grill and put the lid on the barbecue. Smoke-cook for 45 minutes to 1 hour, or until the chicken is well crisped. Brush the chicken with the oil several times during cooking.

Pour the marinade over the chicken and coat evenly with the back of a spoon.

Brush the marinated chicken with the oil several times during cooking.

NUTRITION PER SERVE
Protein 45 g; Fat 11 g; Carbohydrate 3 g; Dietary Fibre 0 g; Cholesterol 100 mg; 1255 kJ (300 Cal)

Teriyaki chicken wings

PREPARATION TIME: 15 MINUTES + 3 HOURS MARINATING | TOTAL COOKING TIME: 15 MINUTES | SERVES 4

8 chicken wings
60 ml (2 fl oz/¼ cup) soy sauce
2 tablespoons dry sherry
2 teaspoons grated fresh ginger
1 garlic clove, crushed
1 tablespoon honey

1 Pat the chicken wings dry with paper towels. Trim any excess fat from the wings, and tuck the tips under to form a triangle.

2 Place the wings in a shallow non-metallic dish. Combine the soy sauce, sherry, ginger, garlic and honey in a bowl, and mix well. Pour the mixture over the chicken wings. Refrigerate, covered, for several hours or overnight. Lightly brush two sheets of aluminium foil with oil. Place 4 wings in a single layer on each piece of foil and wrap completely.

3 Preheat a barbecue grill or flat plate to high. Cook the parcels on the hot barbecue for about 10 minutes. Remove the parcels from the heat and unwrap. Place the wings directly on a lightly greased grill for 3 minutes, or until brown. Turn the wings frequently and brush with any remaining marinade.

NUTRITION PER SERVE
Protein 43 g; Fat 4.5 g; Carbohydrate 6 g; Dietary Fibre 0 g; Cholesterol 95 mg; 998 kJ (238 Cal)

Tuck the tips of the chicken wings under to form a triangle.

Place four chicken wings on each piece of foil and wrap completely.

Place the wings directly on a lightly greased grill and cook until brown.

Middle Eastern baked chicken

PREPARATION TIME: 30 MINUTES + 15 MINUTES SOAKING | TOTAL COOKING TIME: 1 HOUR 30 MINUTES | SERVES 6

1.6 kg (3 lb 8 oz) chicken
95 g (3¼ oz/½ cup) instant couscous
4 pitted dates, chopped
4 dried apricots, chopped
1 tablespoon lime juice
20 g (¾ oz) butter
2 tablespoons olive oil
1 onion, chopped
1–2 garlic cloves, chopped
1 teaspoon ground coriander
2 tablespoons chopped flat-leaf
   (Italian) parsley
¼ teaspoon cracked black pepper
1 teaspoon ground cumin

1 Prepare a kettle barbecue for indirect cooking at medium heat. Place a drip tray underneath the top grill.

2 Remove the giblets and any fat from the chicken. Wipe the chicken with paper towels. Pour 125 ml (4 fl oz/½ cup) boiling water over the couscous and leave to soak for 15 minutes. Soak the dates and apricots in the lime juice and set aside.

3 Heat the butter and half the oil in a saucepan and cook the onion and garlic for 3–4 minutes, or until translucent. Remove from the heat and add the couscous, dates, apricots, coriander, parsley and some salt and pepper. Mix well. Spoon into the chicken cavity and close with a skewer. Tie the legs together with string and tuck the wing tips under.

4 Rub the chicken with the combined salt, cracked black pepper, cumin and remaining oil. Place the chicken in the centre of a large piece of greased foil. Wrap the chicken securely. Place on the barbecue over the drip tray. Cover the barbecue and cook for 50 minutes. Open the foil, crimping the edges to form a tray. Cook for 20 minutes, or until the chicken is tender and golden. Stand for 5–6 minutes before carving. Serve with the stuffing.

NUTRITION PER SERVE
Protein 46 g; Fat 14 g; Carbohydrate 5.5 g; Dietary Fibre 1 g; Cholesterol 110 mg; 1378 kJ (329 Cal)

Remove the giblets and any large deposits of fat from the chicken.

Combine the onion, garlic, couscous, dates, apricots, coriander and parsley and some salt and pepper.

Rub the chicken skin all over with the combined salt, cracked pepper, cumin and remaining oil.

Rice with chicken and seafood

PREPARATION TIME: 40 MINUTES I TOTAL COOKING TIME: 1 HOUR I SERVES 4–6

500 g (1 lb 2 oz) raw medium prawns
500 g (1 lb 2 oz) mussels
200 g (7 oz) squid tubes
60 ml (2 fl oz/¼ cup) olive oil
2 chorizo sausages, thickly sliced
500 g (1 lb 2 oz) chicken pieces
300 g (10½ oz) pork fillet, thickly sliced
4 garlic cloves, crushed
2 red onions, chopped
¼ teaspoon saffron threads, soaked in hot water
¼ teaspoon turmeric
4 large tomatoes, peeled, seeded and chopped
440 g (15½ oz/2 cups) short-grain rice
1.25 litres (44 fl oz/5 cups) hot chicken stock
125 g (4½ oz) green beans, cut into 4 cm
   (1½ inch) lengths
1 red capsicum (pepper), cut into thin strips
155 g (5½ oz/1 cup) fresh peas, shelled

1   Peel the prawns. Devein, leaving the tails intact. Scrub the mussels and remove the beards. Cut the squid tubes into 5 mm (¼ inch) thin slices. Heat 1 tablespoon of the oil in a large frying pan and add the chorizo. Cook over medium heat for 5 minutes, or until browned. Drain. Add the chicken pieces and cook for 5 minutes, or until golden, turning once. Drain.

2   Add the pork to the pan and cook for about 3 minutes, or until browned, turning once. Drain. Heat the remaining oil in the pan, add the garlic, onion, drained saffron and turmeric, cook over medium heat until the onion is soft. Add the tomato and cook for 3 minutes, or until soft.

3   Add the rice and stir until the rice is translucent. Stir in the hot chicken stock, bring to the boil, cover and simmer for 10 minutes. Add the chicken, cover and cook for 20 minutes. Add the pork, prawns, mussels, calamari, chorizo and vegetables. Cover, cook for 10 minutes or until the liquid has been absorbed.

Drain the cooked chorizo sausage slices on paper towels.

Add the rice to the pan and stir for 5 minutes or until the rice is translucent.

NUTRITION PER SERVE (6)
Protein 66 g; Fat 12 g; Carbohydrate 66 g; Dietary Fibre 6 g; Cholesterol 278 mg; 2695 kJ (644 Cal)

Chicken pilaf with spices

PREPARATION TIME: 25 MINUTES I TOTAL COOKING TIME: 40 MINUTES I SERVES 4

1.5 kg (3 lb 5 oz) chicken pieces
80 ml (2½ fl oz/⅓ cup) canola oil
40 g (1½ oz/¼ cup) unblanched
    whole almonds
2 onions, thinly sliced
3 garlic cloves garlic, crushed
1 teaspoon whole black peppercorns
1 teaspoon turmeric
1 teaspoon cumin seeds
2 bay leaves
5 whole cloves
1 cinnamon stick
440 g (15½ oz/2¼ cups) long-grain rice
1 litre (35 fl oz/4 cups) chicken stock
80 g (2¾ oz/½ cup) fresh or frozen peas
30 g (1 oz/¼ cup) sultanas (golden raisins)
3 hard-boiled eggs, peeled and quartered
coriander (cilantro) leaves, to serve

1 Trim the chicken of excess fat and sinew. Heat half the oil in a large frying pan. Add the chicken pieces in batches and cook over medium heat for 5–10 minutes, or until the chicken is brown all over. Drain. Heat 1 tablespoon of the oil in a pan. Add the almonds and cook until the nuts are brown. Remove from the pan and set aside.

2 Heat the remaining oil in a large frying pan. Add the onion and garlic and cook gently over low heat for 2 minutes, stirring occasionally. Add the peppercorns, turmeric, cumin, bay leaves, cloves and cinnamon stick. Fry over high heat for 1 minute, or until fragrant. Stir in the rice, making sure it is well coated with the spices.

3 Add the stock, browned chicken pieces and salt to taste. Bring to the boil, reduce the heat and simmer, covered, for 20 minutes. Add the peas and sultanas and simmer for a further 5 minutes, or until all the liquid is absorbed and the chicken is cooked (you may need to add extra stock or water). Serve with the hard-boiled eggs and sprinkle with the almonds and coriander.

NUTRITION PER SERVE
Protein 67 g; Fat 38 g; Carbohydrate 14 g; Dietary Fibre 4 g; Cholesterol 280 mg; 2755 kJ (658 Cal)

Add the peas and sultanas to the pan and simmer for 5 minutes.

Add the peas and sultanas to the pan and simmer for 5 minutes.

Chicken biryani

PREPARATION TIME: 1 HOUR 30 MINUTES + 4 HOURS MARINATING | TOTAL COOKING TIME: 2 HOURS 45 MINUTES | SERVES 6

MARINADE
6 cardamom pods
3 onions, peeled
3 garlic cloves
5 cm (2 inch) piece fresh ginger, sliced
¼ teaspoon ground cloves
1 teaspoon ground black pepper
1 teaspoon ground cumin
1 teaspoon ground cinnamon
¼ teaspoon ground nutmeg
1½ tablespoons poppy seeds
2 tablespoons lemon juice
250 g (9 oz/1 cup) plain yoghurt

1 kg (2 lb 4 oz) chicken, cut into small pieces
80 ml (2½ fl oz/⅓ cup) oil
3 bay leaves
2 whole cardamom pods, lightly crushed
3 onions, very thinly sliced
2 tablespoons raisins
300 g (10½ oz/1½ cups) long-grain white rice
60 ml (2 fl oz/¼ cup) milk
1 teaspoon sugar
1 teaspoon saffron threads
plain yoghurt, to serve
40 g (1½ oz/¼ cup) toasted cashews, to serve

1 To make the marinade, crush the cardamom pods to release the seeds; discard the pods. Chop the onions, garlic and ginger finely. Add the spices, poppy seeds and lemon juice. Stir in the yoghurt and set aside. Season to taste with salt.

2 Prick the skin of the chicken with a fork (this helps the flavour to infuse into the chicken) and place in a large non-metallic bowl. Add the marinade and evenly coat the chicken, then refrigerate for 4 hours, or overnight.

3 Heat 3 tablespoons of the oil in a frying pan over low heat. Add the bay leaves and cardamom pods and cook for 2 minutes, being careful not to burn. Remove the bay leaves and cardamom and discard. Add the onion and raisins and fry for 8 minutes, or until the onion turn golden. Remove with a slotted spoon, reserving the remaining oil.

4 Place the chicken and the marinade in a flameproof casserole dish and bring to the boil. Cover and simmer for 15 minutes. Remove the chicken with a slotted spoon, leaving as much marinade in the pan as possible. Cook the marinade until reduced to about 250 ml (9 fl oz/1 cup). Return the chicken and toss to coat in the thickened sauce. Set aside.

5 Add the rice to a large saucepan of boiling water and cook for 7 minutes. (Do not cook the rice until tender.) Drain the rice into a sieve. Meanwhile, heat the milk and sugar, pour into a bowl, add the saffron and soak for 5 minutes.

6 Preheat the oven to 150°C (300°F/Gas 2). Pour the saffron mixture over the rice and mix to combine, using a fork. Spoon the rice over the chicken. Pour over the reserved flavoured oil. Cover the dish tightly with foil and bake for 1 hour, or until the rice and chicken are cooked through and tender. Sprinkle with the cashews and serve the yoghurt separately.

NUTRITION PER SERVE
Protein 40 g; Fat 45 g; Carbohydrate 60 g; Dietary Fibre 4 g; Cholesterol 140 mg; 3305 kJ (785 Cal)

Crush the cardamom pods to release the seeds with the flat side of a knife.

Prick the skin of the chicken with a fork to help the flavour infuse into the meat.

Gently streak the saffron mixture through the rice using a fork.

Chicken with olives and sun-dried tomatoes

PREPARATION TIME: 20 MINUTES | TOTAL COOKING TIME: 15 MINUTES | SERVES 4

olive oil, for cooking
4 boneless, skinless chicken breasts, cut
   diagonally into thin slices
1 red onion, thinly sliced
3 garlic cloves, finely chopped
2 tablespoons white wine vinegar
1 teaspoon sambal oelek
1 tablespoon lemon juice
12 Kalamata olives, pitted and quartered
   lengthways
40 g (1½ oz/¼ cup) sun-dried tomatoes,
   cut into thin strips
1 tablespoon shredded basil

1 Heat a wok until very hot, add 2 teaspoons of the oil and swirl it around to coat the side. Stir-fry the chicken slices in two batches until browned and cooked through, adding more oil in between each batch. Remove all the chicken from the wok and keep warm.

2 Reheat the wok, add 1 tablespoon of the oil and stir-fry the onion until it is soft and golden. Add the garlic and cook for 1 minute. Return the warm chicken to the wok. Add the vinegar, sambal oelek and lemon juice, and toss well.

3 Stir in the olive pieces, sun-dried tomato, basil, and season with salt and ground black pepper. Heat through thoroughly.

Sambal oelek is a paste made from salt, vinegar and chilli.

Drain the sun-dried tomatoes and cut them into thin strips.

NUTRITION PER SERVE
Protein 35 g; Fat 15 g; Carbohydrate 2.5 g; Dietary Fibre 1.5 g; Cholesterol 75 mg; 1420 kJ (335 Cal)

Pan-fried chicken tenderloins with vegetables

PREPARATION TIME: 25 MINUTES | TOTAL COOKING TIME: 20 MINUTES | SERVES 4

2 tablespoons olive oil
6 slices prosciutto, cut crossways into
    thin strips
500 g (1 lb 2 oz) chicken tenderloins
1 red onion, chopped
2 garlic cloves, crushed
1 small red chilli, chopped
1 tablespoon plain (all-purpose) flour
375 ml (13 fl oz/1½ cups) chicken stock
150 g (5½ oz) asparagus, halved
250 g (9 oz) green beans, halved
4 tablespoons snipped chives

1   Heat 1 tablespoon of the oil in a frying pan. Stir-fry the prosciutto over medium–high heat for 2 minutes, or until crisp. Lift out with a slotted spoon and drain on paper towels.

2   Add the chicken to the pan and cook over high heat for 2 minutes on each side, or until brown, turning once. Remove from the frying pan and drain on paper towels.

3   Heat the remaining oil in the frying pan. Add the onion, garlic and chilli and stir-fry over medium–high heat for 2 minutes, or until softened. Add the flour and stir for 1 minute.

4   Add the stock gradually, stirring over the heat until the mixture boils and thickens. Add the asparagus and beans and reduce the heat to low. Cook, covered, for 3–5 minutes, or until the vegetables are tender. Return the chicken tenderloins to the pan and cook for 4 minutes, or until the chicken is cooked through. Stir in the snipped chives and serve hot. Sprinkle with the prosciutto.

HINT: *Serve this dish with penne pasta or steamed potatoes.*

Trim the asparagus spears and beans, then cut them in half.

Sprinkle the flour over the onion mixture and stir for 1 minute.

NUTRITION PER SERVE
Protein 4.5 g; Fat 10 g; Carbohydrate 6.5 g; Dietary Fibre 3 g; Cholesterol 2.5 mg; 263 kJ (135 Cal)

Stuffed chicken breast

PREPARATION TIME: 40 MINUTES | TOTAL COOKING TIME: 45 MINUTES | SERVES 6

80 ml (2¾ fl oz/1/3 cup) olive oil
1 onion, finely chopped
2 garlic cloves, crushed
100 g (3½ oz) ham, finely chopped
1 green capsicum (pepper), finely chopped
2 tablespoons finely chopped pitted black
    olives
35 g (1¼ oz/1/3 cup) grated parmesan cheese
6 boneless, skinless chicken breasts
plain (all-purpose) flour, to coat
2 eggs, lightly beaten
150 g (5½ oz/1½ cups) dry breadcrumbs

NUTRITION PER SERVE
Protein 35 g; Fat 20 g; Carbohydrate 20 g; Dietary
Fibre 2 g; Cholesterol 115 mg; 1660 kJ (395 cal)

1 Heat 1 tablespoon of the oil in a saucepan and add the onion, garlic, ham and capsicum. Cook, stirring, over medium heat for 5 minutes, or until the onion is soft. Remove and place in a heatproof bowl. Add the olives and the parmesan cheese.

2 Cut a deep pocket in the side of each chicken breast, cutting almost through to the other side.

3 Fill each breast with the ham mixture and secure with toothpicks along the opening of the pocket. Coat each fillet with the flour, shaking off any excess. Dip into the beaten egg and then coat with the breadcrumbs. Heat the remaining oil in a large frying pan and cook the chicken, in batches, over medium–high heat for 15–20 minutes, turning halfway through, until golden and cooked through. To serve, remove the toothpicks, then cut diagonally into thin slices.

Cut a deep pocket in the side of each breast, cutting almost through to the other side.

Spoon the filling into each breast, securing the pocket openings with toothpicks.

Coat the chicken breasts in the beaten egg and breadcrumbs before cooking.

Pies and roasts

Roast chicken with breadcrumb stuffing

PREPARATION TIME: 40 MINUTES | TOTAL COOKING TIME: 1 HOUR 30 MINUTES | SERVES 6

3 bacon slices, finely chopped
6 slices wholegrain bread, crusts removed
3 spring onions (scallions), chopped
2 tablespoons chopped pecans
2 teaspoons currants
1 handful finely chopped flat-leaf (Italian)
    parsley
1 egg, lightly beaten
60 ml (2 fl oz/¼ cup) milk
1.4 kg (3 lb 12 oz) chicken
40 g (1¼ oz) butter, melted
1 tablespoon oil
1 tablespoon soy sauce
1 garlic clove, crushed
375 ml (13 fl oz/1½ cups) chicken stock
1 tablespoon plain (all-purpose) flour

1 Preheat the oven to 180°C (350°F/ Gas 4). Cook the bacon in a dry frying pan over high heat for 5 minutes, or until crisp. Cut the bread into 1 cm (½ inch) cubes and place in a bowl. Mix in the bacon, spring onion, pecans, currants, parsley and combined egg and milk. Season with salt and freshly ground pepper.

2 Remove the giblets and any large amounts of fat from the cavity of the chicken. Pat the chicken dry with paper towels. Spoon the bacon mixture into the chicken cavity. Tuck the wing tips under the chicken and tie the legs securely with string.

3 Place the chicken on a rack in a deep baking dish. Brush with the combined butter, oil and soy sauce. Pour any remaining mixture into the baking dish with the garlic and half the stock. Roast the chicken for 1–1¼ hours, or until brown and tender, basting occasionally with the pan juices. Pierce the thighs and check that any juices running out are clear. If they are pink, continue cooking. Cover the chicken loosely with foil and leave in a warm place for 5 minutes before carving.

4 Discard all but 1 tablespoon of the pan juices from the baking dish. Transfer the baking dish to the stove. Add the flour to the pan juices and blend to a smooth paste. Stir constantly over low heat for 5 minutes, or until the mixture browns. Gradually add the remaining stock and stir until the mixture boils and thickens. Add a little extra stock or water if needed. Season and strain into a jug. Serve the chicken with the sauce.

NUTRITION PER SERVE
Protein 33 g; Fat 20 g; Carbohydrate 15 g; Dietary Fibre 3 g; Cholesterol 110 mg; 1530 kJ (365 Cal)

Pat the chicken dry and spoon the stuffing into the chicken cavity.

Tuck the wing tips under the chicken and tie the legs securely with string.

Chicken with redcurrant sauce

PREPARATION TIME: 25 MINUTES + 2 HOURS MARINATING I TOTAL COOKING TIME: 30 MINUTES I SERVES 4

4 chicken leg quarters (marylands)
125 ml (4 fl oz/½ cup) red wine
1 tablespoon finely chopped thyme
1 tablespoon finely chopped rosemary,
   some extra, to serve
1 tablespoon olive oil
160 g (5½ oz/½ cup) redcurrant jelly

1 Trim the chicken of excess fat and sinew. Place the chicken in a shallow non-metallic dish. Combine the wine, thyme and rosemary in a small bowl and pour over the chicken. Refrigerate, covered, for 2 hours or overnight, turning the chicken occasionally.

2 Preheat the oven to 200°C (400°F/Gas 6). Drain the chicken and reserve the marinade. Place the chicken in a baking dish and brush with the oil. Bake for 30 minutes, or until cooked through, turning occasionally.

3 Meanwhile, combine the reserved marinade and redcurrant jelly in a small saucepan. Stir over medium heat until smooth, then bring to the boil. Reduce the heat and simmer, uncovered, for 15 minutes. Pour the sauce over the chicken and sprinkle with rosemary.

Pour the wine, thyme and rosemary mixture over the chicken leg quarters.

Combine the reserved marinade and redcurrant jelly in a small saucepan and stir until smooth.

NUTRITION PER SERVE
Protein 37 g; Fat 8.5 g; Carbohydrate 5 g; Dietary Fibre 0 g; Cholesterol 90 mg; 1112 kJ (266 Cal)

Orange roasted chickens

PREPARATION TIME: 15 MINUTES + 3 HOURS MARINATING | TOTAL COOKING TIME: 40 MINUTES | SERVES 8

2 x 800 g (1 lb 12 oz) chickens
100 g (3½ oz) butter, softened
2 garlic cloves, crushed
1 tablespoon finely grated orange zest
60 ml (2 fl oz/¼ cup) orange juice

1 Using kitchen scissors, cut the chickens in half through the backbone and breastbone. Pat dry with paper towels and wipe the inside.

2 Combine the butter, garlic and orange zest and beat well. Gently loosen the skin of the chickens by sliding your fingers between the flesh and the skin. Push the orange butter under the skin as evenly as possible. Put the chickens in a non-metallic dish and pour over the orange juice. Cover and refrigerate for 3 hours, or preferably overnight.

3 Preheat the oven to 220°C (425°F/Gas 7). Drain the chicken pieces well and arrange cut side down on roasting racks inside two baking dishes. Pour 2 tablespoons of water into each baking dish.

4 Roast for 30–40 minutes, or until the chickens are golden brown. Cover with foil and allow to rest for 15 minutes. Cut into quarters to serve.

NOTE: *For the best result, use freshly squeezed orange juice.*

NUTRITION PER SERVE
Protein 30 g; Fat 15 g; Carbohydrate 1 g; Dietary
Fibre 0 g; Cholesterol 95 mg; 990 kJ (235 Cal)

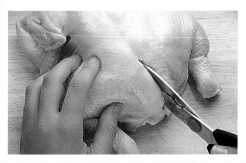

Cut the chickens in half through the backbone and breastbone.

Loosen the skin of the chickens and spread the orange butter underneath.

Chicken and leek cobbler

PREPARATION TIME: 1 HOUR I TOTAL COOKING TIME: 1 HOUR I SERVES 4–6

50 g (1¾ oz) butter

1 kg (2 lb 4 oz) boneless, skinless chicken breasts, cut into thick strips

1 large (225 g/8 oz) leek, trimmed and thinly sliced

1 celery stalk, thinly sliced

1 tablespoon plain (all-purpose) flour

250 ml (9 fl oz/1 cup) chicken stock

250 ml (9 fl oz/1 cup) cream

3 teaspoons dijon mustard

3 teaspoons drained and rinsed green peppercorns

TOPPING

400 g (14 oz) potatoes, quartered

165 g (5¾ oz/1⅓ cups) self-raising flour

½ teaspoon salt

30 g (1 oz/¼ cup) grated mature cheddar cheese

100 g (3½ oz) cold butter, chopped

1 egg yolk, lightly beaten, to glaze

1 tablespoon milk, to glaze

NUTRITION PER SERVE (6)
Protein 45 g; Fat 30 g; Carbohydrate 30 g; Dietary Fibre 4 g; Cholesterol 185 mg; 2405 kJ (570 Cal)

1   Melt half the butter in a pan. When it begins to foam, add the chicken and cook until golden. Remove from the pan. Add the remaining butter and cook the leek and celery over medium heat until soft. Return the chicken to the pan.

2   Sprinkle the flour over the chicken and stir for about 1 minute. Remove from the heat and stir in the stock and cream. Mix well, making sure that there are no lumps. Return to the heat. Bring to the boil, then reduce the heat and simmer for about 20 minutes. Add the mustard, and peppercorns and season. Transfer the mixture to a 1.25–1.5 litre (45–52 fl oz/ 5–6 cup) capacity casserole dish and allow to cool. Preheat the oven to 200°C (400°F/Gas 6).

3   To make the topping, cook the potato in a saucepan of boiling water until tender. Drain and mash until smooth. Place the flour and salt in a food processor and add the cheese and butter. Process in short bursts until the mixture forms crumbs. Add this mixture to the mashed potato and bring together to form a dough.

4   Roll out the dough on a lightly floured surface, until it is 1 cm (½ inch) thick. Cut into circles with a 6 cm (2½ inch) diameter pastry cutter. Keep re-rolling the pastry scraps until all the dough is used. Arrange circles on top of the cooled chicken and leek filling.

5   Brush the dough with the combined egg yolk and milk. Bake for 30 minutes, or until heated through and the pastry is golden.

Add the mustard and peppercorns to the simmering chicken and leek mixture.

Bring together the crumb mixture and mashed potato with your hands.

Arrange the circles, overlapping, on top of the cooled chicken and leek mixture.

Chicken and mushroom pithivier

PREPARATION TIME: 45 MINUTES + 30 MINUTES REFRIGERATION | TOTAL COOKING TIME: 40 MINUTES | SERVES 4

50 g (1¾ oz) butter
2 bacon slices, chopped
4 spring onions (scallions), chopped
100 g (3½ oz) button mushrooms, sliced
1 tablespoon plain (all-purpose) flour
185 ml (6 fl oz/¾ cup) milk
1 tablespoon thick cream
180 g (6 oz/1 cup) chopped cooked chicken
    breast
1 handul chopped flat-leaf (Italian) parsley
2 sheets ready-rolled puff pastry
1 egg yolk, lightly beaten, to glaze

1   Melt the butter in a frying pan and cook the bacon and spring onion, stirring, for 2–3 minutes. Add the mushrooms and cook, stirring, for 3 minutes. Stir in the flour and cook for 1 minute. Add the milk all at once and stir for 2–3 minutes, or until thickened. Simmer for 1 minute, then remove from the heat. Stir in the cream, chicken and parsley. Set aside to cool.

2   Cut two 23 cm (9 inch) circles from the pastry sheets, using a dinner plate or cake tin as a guide. Place 1 circle on a greased baking tray. Pile the chicken filling into the centre of the pastry, mounding slightly in the centre and leaving a 2 cm (¾ inch) border. Combine the egg yolk with 1 teaspoon of water, and brush the pastry border.

3   Using a small pointed knife, and starting from the centre of the second circle, mark curved lines at regular intervals. Take care not to cut through the pastry. Place this sheet over the other and stretch a little to fit evenly. Press the edges together to seal. Using the back of a knife, push up the outside edge at 1 cm (½ inch) intervals. Cover and refrigerate for at least 30 minutes. Preheat the oven to 190°C (375°F/Gas 5). Brush the pastry with the egg mixture and make a small hole in the centre for steam to escape. Bake for 25 minutes, or until golden.

Draw curved lines from the centre of the edge of the pastry.

Use the back of a knife to push up the edge of the pastry.

NUTRITION PER SERVE
Protein 25 g; Fat 40 g; Carbohydrate 35 g; Dietary Fibre 2 g; Cholesterol 160 mg; 2395 kJ (570 Cal)

Family chicken pie

PREPARATION TIME: 40 MINUTES + 20 MINUTES REFRIGERATION | TOTAL COOKING TIME: 1 HOUR | SERVES 6

PASTRY
250 g (9 oz/2 cups) self-raising flour
125 g (4½ oz/½ cup) butter, chopped
1 egg

FILLING
1 barbecued chicken
30 g (1 oz) butter
1 onion, finely chopped
310 g (11 oz) tinned creamed corn
310 ml (10¾ fl oz/1¼ cups) cream

1   To make the pastry, process the flour and butter in a food processor for 15 seconds, or until the mixture is fine and crumbly. Add the egg and 2–3 tablespoons water and process for 30 seconds, or until the mixture just comes together. Turn onto a lightly floured surface and gather together into a smooth ball. Cover with plastic wrap and refrigerate for 20 minutes.

2   Meanwhile, to make the filling, remove the meat from the chicken carcass and shred finely. Heat the butter in a frying pan and cook the onion over medium heat for 3 minutes. Add the chicken, corn and cream. Bring to the boil, then reduce the heat and simmer for 10 minutes. Remove from the heat and allow to cool slightly.

3   Preheat the oven to 180°C (350°F/Gas 4). Roll half the pastry between two sheets of plastic wrap to cover the base and side of a 23 cm (9 inch) pie dish. Spoon the chicken mixture into the pastry-lined dish.

4   Roll the remaining pastry to cover the top of the pie. Brush with milk. Press the edges together to seal. Trim the edges with a sharp knife. Roll the excess pastry into two long ropes and twist together. Brush the pie edge with a little milk and place the pastry rope around the rim. Bake for 45 minutes or until pastry is golden.

NUTRITION PER SERVE
Protein 18 g; Fat 48 g; Carbohydrate 44 g; Dietary Fibre 4 g; Cholesterol 212 mg; 2832 kJ (676 Cal)

Roll half the pastry out between two sheets of plastic wrap.

Brush the pie edge with a little milk, then place the pastry rope around the rim of the pie.

Thai green curry chicken pies

PREPARATION TIME: 45 MINUTES + 30 MINUTES REFRIGERATION | TOTAL COOKING TIME: 45 MINUTES | SERVES 4

125 g (4½ oz/1 cup) plain (all-purpose) flour
65 g (2¼ oz) cold butter, chopped

FILLING
1 tablespoon vegetable oil
1 tablespoon Thai green curry paste
125 ml (4 fl oz/½ cup) coconut milk
500 g (1 lb 2 oz) boneless, skinless chicken
    thighs, cut into bite-sized pieces
200 g (7 oz) green beans, cut into short
    lengths
2 makrut (kaffir lime) leaves
2 teaspoons fish sauce
1 tablespoon lime juice
2 teaspoons soft brown sugar
1 tablespoon cornflour (cornstarch)
1 egg, lightly beaten, to glaze

1   Process the flour and butter in a food processor until the mixture resembles fine breadcrumbs. Add 1–2 tablespoons of cold water. Process in short bursts until the mixture just comes together, adding a little extra water if necessary. Turn out onto a lightly floured surface and quickly bring together into a ball. Cover with plastic wrap and refrigerate for at least 30 minutes.

2   Heat the oil in a wok or heavy-based frying pan. Add the curry paste and cook for 1 minute, stirring constantly. Add the coconut milk and 60 ml (2 fl oz/¼ cup) water and bring to the boil. Add the chicken, beans and makrut leaves and stir through. Simmer for 15 minutes, or until the chicken is cooked. Add the fish sauce, lime juice and sugar. Mix together the cornflour and 1 tablespoon of water to a smooth consistency. Add to the curry and stir constantly until the sauce thickens and begins to bubble. Remove the makrut leaves, and divide the mixture between four 125 ml (4 fl oz/½ cup) capacity ramekins.

3   Divide the pastry into 4 equal pieces. Roll each piece between two sheets of baking paper until it is slightly larger than the top of the ramekins. Brush the edges of the ramekins with the beaten egg and cover with the pastry. Press the edges around the rim to seal. Trim off any excess pastry with a knife. Cut a small air hole in the top of each pie to allow the steam to escape during cooking. Brush with the beaten egg. Place the ramekins on a baking tray and bake for 20–25 minutes, or until the pastry is golden brown. Serve immediately.

NUTRITION PER SERVE
Protein 35 g; Fat 30 g; Carbohydrate 30 g; Dietary Fibre 3 g; Cholesterol 175 mg; 2225 kJ (530 Cal)

Cook the curry paste for 1 minute, then add the coconut milk.

Add the cornflour mixture to the curry and stir until it thickens and bubbles.

Roll out each piece of pastry and place over the top of the ramekins.

Mustard chicken and asparagus quiche

PREPARATION TIME: 25 MINUTES + 40 MINUTES REFRIGERATION | TOTAL COOKING TIME: 1 HOUR 20 MINUTES | SERVES 8

250 g (9 oz/2 cups) plain (all-purpose) flour
100 g (3½ oz) cold butter, chopped
1 egg yolk

FILLING
150 g (5½ oz) asparagus, chopped
25 g (1 oz) butter
1 onion, chopped
60 g (2¼ oz/¼ cup) wholegrain mustard
200 g (7 oz) soft cream cheese
125 ml (4 fl oz/½ cup) cream
3 eggs, lightly beaten
200 g (7 oz) cooked chicken, chopped

1   Process the flour and butter until crumbly. Add the egg yolk and 3 tablespoons of water. Process in short bursts until the mixture comes together. Add a little extra water if needed. Gather dough into a ball on a floured surface. Cover with plastic wrap and chill for 30 minutes. Grease a 19 cm (7½ inch) diameter deep loose-based flan tin.

2   Roll out the pastry and line the tin. Trim off any excess. Place the tin on a baking tray and chill for 10 minutes. Preheat the oven to 200°C (400°F/Gas 6). Cover the pastry with baking paper and fill evenly with baking beads. Bake for 10 minutes. Remove the paper and beads and bake for about 10 minutes, or until the pastry is lightly browned and dry. Cool. Reduce the oven to 180°C (350°F/Gas 4).

3   To make the filling, steam the asparagus until tender. Drain and pat dry. Melt the butter in a saucepan over low heat and cook the onion until soft. Remove from the heat and add the mustard and cream cheese, stirring until the cheese has melted. Cool. Add the cream, eggs, chicken and asparagus and mix well. Spoon the filling into the pastry shell and season. Bake for 50 minutes to 1 hour, or until puffed and set. Cool for 15 minutes before cutting.

When the flour and butter mixture is crumbly, add the egg yolk.

Pat dry the asparagus well with paper towel to prevent excess moisture from softening the quiche.

NUTRITION PER SERVE
Protein 15 g; Fat 30 g; Carbohydrate 25 g; Dietary Fibre 2 g; Cholesterol 190 mg; 1860 kJ (440 Cal)

Baked chicken and artichoke pancakes

PREPARATION TIME: 30 MINUTES | TOTAL COOKING TIME: 1 HOUR | SERVES 4

1 teaspoon baking powder

165 g (5¾ oz/1⅓ cups) plain (all-purpose) flour

¼ teaspoon salt

2 eggs

300 ml (10½ fl oz) milk

90 g (3¼ oz/⅓ cup) butter, melted,
    extra, to grease

600 ml (21 fl oz) chicken stock

2 egg yolks, lightly whisked

250 ml (9 fl oz/1 cup) cream

1 teaspoon lemon juice

300 g (10½ oz) cooked chicken, chopped

350 g (12 oz) tinned artichoke hearts, drained
    and sliced

2 teaspoons chopped parsley

100 g (3½ oz/1 cup) grated parmesan cheese

1 Sift the baking powder, 125 g (4 oz/1 cup) of the flour and salt into a bowl, make a well in the centre and whisk in the eggs and milk until just smooth. Heat a frying pan and brush with butter. Add 60 ml (2 fl oz/¼ cup) batter and cook over medium heat until the underside is brown. Turn over and cook the other side. Transfer to a plate and cover while cooking the remaining batter.

2 Put the butter in a frying pan and stir in the remaining flour. Cook for 2 minutes, then remove from the heat. Whisk in the stock until smooth. Whisk in the combined egg yolks and cream and bring slowly to the boil, stirring constantly. Boil for 30 seconds until the sauce thickens, remove from the heat and stir in the lemon juice. Season with salt and pepper.

3 Preheat the oven to 200°C (400°F/Gas 6). Grease a 3 litre (10 fl oz/12 cups) capacity ovenproof dish with butter. Line the base with 2 pancakes, slightly overlapping. Spoon half of the filling evenly over the pancakes. Pour a third of the sauce over the top and layer with 2 pancakes. Repeat, finishing with a layer of 3 pancakes. Spread the remaining sauce over, sprinkle with parmesan and bake for 30–35 minutes.

NUTRITION PER SERVE
Protein 40 g; Fat 60 g; Carbohydrate 37 g; Dietary Fibre 4 g; Cholesterol 305 mg; 3568 kJ (850 Cal)

Heat a frying pan, add the batter and cook until the underside is brown.

Line the dish with pancakes, then spoon in half the chicken and artichoke filling.

Chicken ballotine

PREPARATION TIME: 40 MINUTES | TOTAL COOKING TIME: 1 HOUR 45 MINUTES | SERVES 8

1.6 kg (3 lb 8 oz) chicken
2 red capsicums (peppers)
1 kg (2 lb 4 oz/1 bunch) silverbeet
30 g (1 oz) butter
1 onion, finely chopped
1 garlic clove, crushed
50 g (1¾ oz/½ cup) grated parmesan cheese
80 g (2¾ oz/1 cup) fresh breadcrumbs
1 tablespoon chopped oregano
200 g (7 oz) ricotta cheese

1 To bone the chicken, cut through the skin on the centre back with a sharp knife. Separate the flesh from the bone down one side to the breast, being careful not to pierce the skin. Follow along the bones closely with the knife, gradually easing the meat from the thigh, drumstick and wing. Cut through the thigh bone where it meets the drumstick and cut off the wing tip. Repeat on the other side, then lift the ribcage away, leaving the flesh in one piece and the drumsticks still attached to the flesh. Scrape all the meat from the drumsticks and wings, discarding the bones. Turn the wing and drumstick flesh inside the chicken and lay the chicken out flat, skin side down. Refrigerate.

2 Preheat the oven to 180°C (350°F/Gas 4). Quarter the capsicums, remove the membranes and seeds. Place skin side up under a hot grill until the skin blackens. Place in a plastic bag and allow to cool, then peel off the skin.

3 Remove the stalks from the silverbeet and finely shred the leaves. Melt the butter in a large frying pan and add the onion and garlic. Cook for about 5 minutes, or until soft. Add the silverbeet leaves and stir until wilted and all the moisture has evaporated. In a food processor, process the silverbeet and onion mixture with the parmesan, breadcrumbs, oregano and half the ricotta. Season to taste.

4 Spread the silverbeet mixture over the chicken and lay the capsicum over the silverbeet. Form the remaining ricotta into a roll and place across the width of the chicken. Fold the sides of the chicken in over the filling so they overlap slightly, and tuck the ends in neatly. Roll the chicken up to enclose the filling and secure with toothpicks and tie with string at 3 cm (1¼ inch) intervals.

5 Lightly grease a large piece of aluminium foil and place the chicken in the centre. Roll the chicken up securely in the foil, sealing the ends well. Place on a baking tray and bake for 1¼–1½ hours, or until the juices run clear when a skewer is inserted into the centre. Allow to cool, then refrigerate until cold before removing the foil, toothpicks and string. Cut into 1 cm (½ inch) slices to serve.

NOTE: *If you are not confident about boning a chicken, ask your butcher to do it for you. To be on the safe side, it might be worth ordering your boned chicken a day in advance.*

NUTRITION PER SERVE
Protein 40 g; Fat 12 g; Carbohydrate 9 g; Dietary Fibre 1.5 g; Cholesterol 105 mg; 1290 kJ (310 Cal)

Using a sharp knife, cut through the skin on the centre back.

Lay the chicken out flat and cover with the silverbeet mixture and capsicum quarters.

Roll the chicken up to enclose the filling and secure with toothpicks.

Roast garlic chicken with vegetables

PREPARATION TIME: 20 MINUTES | TOTAL COOKING TIME: 1 HOUR 15 MINUTES | SERVES 4

310 g (11 oz) orange sweet potatoes, peeled and cut into wedges

310 g (11 oz) pontiac potatoes, peeled and cut into wedges

310 g (11 oz) pumpkin (winter squash), peeled and cut into wedges

1 chicken, cut into 8 pieces, or 1.5 kg (3 lb 5 oz) chicken pieces

60 ml (2 fl oz/¼ cup) olive oil

1 tablespoon thyme

20 large garlic cloves, unpeeled (see NOTE)

½ teaspoon sea salt

1   Preheat the oven to 220°C (425°F/Gas 7). Put the chicken and vegetables in a baking dish, drizzle with the olive oil and scatter with the thyme leaves and garlic cloves. Sprinkle with the sea salt.

2   Roast for 1 hour 15 minutes, turning every 20 minutes, or until the chicken, sweet potato, potato and pumpkin are well browned and crisp at the edges. Serve immediately.

NOTE: *This may seem an awful lot of garlic, but it loses its pungency when roasted, becoming sweet and mild. To eat the garlic, squeeze the creamy roasted flesh from the skins and over the chicken and vegetables.*

Drizzle the chicken and vegetables with oil, then sprinkle with garlic and thyme.

Turn the chicken pieces and vegetables every 20 minutes, until browned and crisp.

NUTRITION PER SERVE
Protein 35 g; Fat 20 g; Carbohydrate 28 g; Dietary Fibre 6 g; Cholesterol 97 mg; 1848 kJ (440 Cal)

Chicken with baked eggplant and tomato

PREPARATION TIME: 30 MINUTES | TOTAL COOKING TIME: 1 HOUR 30 MINUTES | SERVES 4

1 red capsicum (pepper)

1 eggplant (aubergine)

3 tomatoes, cut into quarters

200 g (7 oz) large button mushrooms, halved

1 onion, cut into thin wedges

cooking oil spray

1½ tablespoons tomato paste (concentrated purée)

125 ml (4 fl oz/½ cup) chicken stock

60 ml (2 fl oz/¼ cup) white wine

2 lean bacon slices

4 boneless, skinless chicken breasts

4 small rosemary sprigs

1   Preheat the oven to 200°C (400°F/Gas 6). Cut the capsicum and eggplant into bite-sized pieces and combine with the tomato, mushrooms and onion in a baking dish. Spray with oil and bake for 1 hour, or until starting to brown and soften, stirring once.

2   Pour the combined tomato paste, stock and wine into the dish and bake for 10 minutes, or until thickened.

3   Meanwhile, discard the fat and rind from the bacon and cut in half. Wrap a strip of bacon around each chicken breast and secure it underneath with a toothpick. Poke a sprig of fresh rosemary underneath the bacon. Pan-fry in a lightly oiled, non-stick frying pan over medium heat until golden on both sides. Cover and cook for 10–15 minutes, or until the chicken is tender and cooked through. Remove the toothpicks. Serve the chicken on the vegetable mixture, surrounded with the sauce.

NUTRITION PER SERVE
Protein 35 g; Fat 4.5 g; Carbohydrate 8 g; Dietary Fibre 5 g; Cholesterol 70 mg; 965 kJ (230 Cal)

When the vegetables have softened, add the combined tomato paste, stock and wine.

Wrap a strip of bacon around the chicken and secure with a toothpick.

Chicken and sugar snap pea parcels

PREPARATION TIME: 40 MINUTES | TOTAL COOKING TIME: 30 MINUTES | SERVES 8

200 g (7 oz) sugar snap peas (mangetouts)

1 tablespoon vegetable oil

6 boneless, skinless chicken thighs, cut into
    1 cm (½ inch) thick strips

40 g (1½ oz) butter

2 tablespoons plain (all-purpose) flour

185 ml (6½ fl oz/¾ cup) chicken stock

170 ml (5½ fl oz/⅔ cup) dry white wine

1 tablespoon wholegrain mustard

150 g (5½ oz) feta cheese, cut into 1 cm
    (½ inch) cubes

50 g (1¾ oz/⅓ cup) sliced sun-dried
    tomatoes, finely chopped

24 sheets filo pastry

60 g (2¼ oz/⅓ cup) butter, extra, melted

sesame and sunflower seeds

1 Preheat the oven to 210°C (415°F/Gas 6–7). Top and tail the sugar snap peas, then plunge into boiling water for 1 minute, or until bright in colour but still crunchy. Drain well.

2 Heat the oil in a heavy-based frying pan. Cook the chicken quickly, in small batches, over medium heat until well browned. Remove and drain on paper towels.

3 Melt the butter in the saucepan and add the flour. Stir over low heat for 2 minutes, or until the flour mixture is light golden and bubbling. Add the stock, wine and mustard, stirring until the mixture is smooth. Stir constantly over medium heat until the mixture boils and thickens. Stir in the chicken, sugar snap peas, feta and tomato and mix gently. Remove from the heat and allow to cool. Divide the mixture evenly into eight portions.

4 Brush three sheets of the pastry with the melted butter. Place the sheets on top of each other. Place one portion of the mixture at one short end of the pastry. Roll and fold the pastry, enclosing the filling to form a parcel. Brush with a little more butter and place seam side down on a greased baking tray. Repeat with the remaining pastry, butter and filling. Brush the tops with butter. Sprinkle with the sesame and sunflower seeds. Bake for 20 minutes, or until golden brown and cooked through. Serve with a mixed green leaf salad.

NUTRITION PER SERVE
Protein 34 g; Fat 20 g; Carbohydrate 20 g; Dietary Fibre 2 g; Cholesterol 100 mg; 1720 kJ (410 Cal)

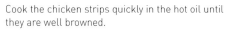

Cook the chicken strips quickly in the hot oil until they are well browned.

Place one portion of mixture on the pastry and roll up, enclosing the filling to form a parcel.

Chicken coriander pie

PREPARATION TIME: 40 MINUTES | TOTAL COOKING TIME: 45 MINUTES | SERVES 4

50 g (1¾ oz) butter
2 onions, chopped
100 g (3½ oz) button mushrooms, sliced
250 g (9 oz) cooked chicken, roughly chopped
4 hard-boiled eggs
1 tablespoon plain (all-purpose) flour
290 ml (10 fl oz) chicken stock
1 egg yolk
4 tablespoons chopped coriander
(cilantro) leaves
250 g (9 oz) block or packet puff pastry
1 egg, lightly beaten, to glaze

1 Melt half of the butter in a large frying pan. Add the onion and mushrooms and sauté for about 5 minutes, or until soft, then stir in the chicken. Spoon half of the mixture into a 20 cm (8 inch) round, straight-sided pie dish. Slice the eggs and lay over the chicken. Top with the remaining mixture.

2 Preheat the oven to 200°C (400°F/Gas 6). Melt the remaining butter in a saucepan, add the flour and cook for 1 minute. Gradually add the stock and cook for 4 minutes, stirring constantly, then remove from the heat. Stir in the egg yolk and coriander, and season with salt and ground black pepper. Allow the mixture to cool before pouring over the chicken filling.

3 Roll out the pastry into a square larger than the pie dish. Dampen the dish rim with water and lay the pastry over, pressing down firmly to seal. Trim the edges and roll out the leftover pastry into a long strip. Slice it into 3 equal lengths and make a plait. Brush the top of the pie with beaten egg and place the plait around the edge. Brush again with beaten egg. Make a few slits in the centre and bake for 35 minutes, or until golden.

Slice the hard-boiled eggs and arrange them over the chicken filling.

Stir the egg yolk and coriander into the heated stock and flour.

NUTRITION PER SERVE
Protein 25 g; Fat 35 g; Carbohydrate 30 g; Dietary Fibre 3 g; Cholesterol 385 mg; 2220 kJ (530 Cal)

Moroccan chicken filo pie

PREPARATION TIME: 40 MINUTES | TOTAL COOKING TIME: 40 MINUTES | SERVES 4–6

1 tablespoon olive oil
1 red onion, chopped
2–3 garlic cloves, crushed
2 teaspoons grated fresh ginger
1 teaspoon ground turmeric
1 teaspoon ground cumin
1 teaspoon ground coriander
500 g (1 lb 2 oz) cooked chicken, shredded
60 g (2¼ oz/½ cup) slivered almonds, toasted
1 handful chopped coriander (cilantro) leaves
4 tablespoons chopped parsley
1 teaspoon grated lemon zest
2 tablespoons chicken stock or water
1 egg, lightly beaten
9 sheets filo pastry
50 g (1¾ oz) butter, melted
1 teaspoon caster (superfine) sugar
¼ teaspoon ground cinnamon

1 Heat the oil in a frying pan and cook the onion, garlic and ginger, stirring, for 5 minutes, or until the onion is soft. Stir in the turmeric, cumin and coriander and cook, stirring, for 1–2 minutes. Remove from the heat and stir in the chicken, almonds, coriander, parsley and lemon zest. Leave to cool for 5 minutes, then stir in the stock or water and the beaten egg.

2 Preheat the oven to 180°C (350°F/Gas 4). Grease a baking tray. Cut 6 sheets of filo into approximately 30 cm (12 inch) squares, retaining the extra strips. Cut each of the remaining sheets into 3 equal strips. Cover with a damp tea towel. Brush 1 square with the butter and place on the baking tray. Lay another square at an angle on top and brush with the butter. Repeat with the other squares to form a rough 8-pointed star. Spoon the chicken mixture into the centre, leaving a 5 cm (2 inch) border. Turn the pastry edge in, leaving the centre open. Brush the pastry strips with the butter and lightly scrunch, lay them over the top of the pie. Sprinkle with the sugar and cinnamon. Bake for 25 minutes.

NUTRITION PER SERVE (6)
Protein 30 g; Fat 20 g; Carbohydrate 15 g; Dietary Fibre 2 g; Cholesterol 130 mg; 1510 kJ (360 Cal)

Gather the edges of the pastry squares up over the chicken mixture.

Lightly scrunch the remaining pastry strips and arrange them around the pie top.

Low-fat chicken pies

PREPARATION TIME: 50 MINUTES + 30 MINUTES REFRIGERATION | TOTAL COOKING TIME: 1 HOUR 10 MINUTES | SERVES 4

300 g (10½ oz) boneless, skinless
   chicken breasts
1 bay leaf
500 ml (17 fl oz/2 cups) chicken stock
2 large potatoes, chopped
250 g (9 oz) orange sweet potato, chopped
2 celery stalks, chopped
2 carrots, chopped
1 onion, chopped
1 parsnip, chopped
1 garlic clove, crushed
1 tablespoon cornflour (cornstarch)
250 ml (9 fl oz/1 cup) skim milk
155 g (5½ oz/1 cup) frozen peas, thawed
1 tablespoon snipped chives
1 tablespoon chopped parsley
185 g (6½ oz/1½ cups) self-raising flour
20 g (¾ oz) butter
80 ml (2½ fl oz/⅓ cup) milk
1 egg, lightly beaten
½ teaspoon sesame seeds

1 Combine the chicken, bay leaf and stock in a large non-stick frying pan and simmer over low heat for 10 minutes, until the chicken is cooked through. Remove the chicken, cool, then cut into small pieces. Add the potato, orange sweet potato, celery and carrot to the pan and simmer, covered, for about 10 minutes, or until just tender. Remove the vegetables with a slotted spoon.

2 Add the onion, parsnip and garlic to the pan and simmer, uncovered, for about 10 minutes, or until very soft. Discard the bay leaf. Purée the mixture in a food processor until smooth.

3 Stir the cornflour into 2 tablespoons of the skim milk until it forms a smooth paste. Stir the cornflour mixture into the puréed mixture with the remaining milk, return to the frying pan. Stir over low heat until the mixture boils and thickens. Preheat the oven to 200°C (400°F/Gas 6).

4 Combine the puréed mixture with the remaining vegetables, chicken and herbs. Season with salt and pepper. Spoon into four 435 ml (15½ fl oz/1¾ cups) ovenproof dishes.

5 To make the pastry, sift the flour into a large bowl, rub in the butter with your fingertips, then make a well in the centre. Combine the milk with 80 ml (2½ fl oz/⅓ cup)

water and add enough to the dry ingredients to make a soft dough. Turn out onto a lightly floured surface and knead until just smooth. Cut the dough into four portions and roll each out, 1 cm (½ inch) larger than the top of the dish.

6 Brush the edge of the dough with the egg, then press it over the top of each dish to seal. Brush the pastry with the remaining egg and sprinkle with the sesame seeds. Bake for about 30 minutes, or until golden and the filling is heated through.

NUTRITION PER SERVE
Protein 30 g; Fat 10 g; Carbohydrate 65 g; Dietary Fibre 9.5 g; Cholesterol 100 mg; 2045 kJ (490 Cal)

Simmer the chicken with the bay leaf and stock until cooked through.

Add enough liquid to the dry ingredients to make a soft dough.

Brush the edges of the dough with egg, then press a portion over the top of each dish.

Roast chicken with country sage stuffing

PREPARATION TIME: 25 MINUTES | TOTAL COOKING TIME: 1 HOUR 40 MINUTES | SERVES 4

1.5 kg (3 lb 5 oz) chicken
45 g (1½ oz) butter
1 onion, finely chopped
1 celery stalk, thinly sliced
160 g (5½ oz/2 cups) fresh white breadcrumbs
½ teaspoon white pepper
10 large sage leaves, shredded or
    1½ teaspoons dried sage
4 tablespoons finely chopped parsley
2 egg whites, lightly beaten
30 g (1 oz) butter, melted
1 tablespoon plain (all-purpose) flour

1   Preheat the oven to 180°C (350°F/Gas 4).
Remove the giblets and any large fat deposits
from the chicken. Wipe the chicken and pat dry
with paper towels. Tuck the wing tips under the
chicken. Grease a large shallow baking dish.

2   Heat the butter in a saucepan. Add the onion
and celery and cook for 3–4 minutes, or until the
onion is soft. Transfer the mixture to a bowl, add
the breadcrumbs, salt, pepper, sage, parsley and
egg whites. The stuffing should be very moist.

3   Spoon the stuffing into the chicken cavity
and close with a skewer or toothpick. Tie the
wings and drumsticks with string. Brush the
chicken all over with the melted butter. Place the
chicken in the baking dish. Bake for 1½ hours,
basting occasionally. Cook until the juices run
clear, when the thigh is pierced with a skewer.
Transfer the chicken to a serving dish, cover and
let stand for 10 minutes before carving.

4   Meanwhile, to make the gravy, transfer the
baking dish to the stovetop. Add the flour to
the pan juices and blend to a smooth paste. Stir
constantly over low heat for 5 minutes, or until
the gravy boils and thickens. If the gravy is too
thick, add a little water or chicken stock. Season.
Serve the chicken with the gravy and stuffing.

Close and secure the chicken cavity, and tie the
drumsticks securely with string.

Transfer the baking dish to the stovetop and
sprinkle with flour.

NUTRITION PER SERVE
Protein 70 g; Fat 30 g; Carbohydrate 33 g; Dietary
Fibre 2.5 g; Cholesterol 255 mg; 2865 kJ (684 Cal)

Spring chicken with honey glaze

PREPARATION TIME: 15 MINUTES | TOTAL COOKING TIME: 55 MINUTES | SERVES 6–8

2 small (1.5 kg/3 lb 5 oz) chickens
1 tablespoon light olive oil

HONEY GLAZE
90 g (3¼ oz/¼ cup) honey
juice and finely grated zest of 1 lemon
1 tablespoon finely chopped rosemary
1 tablespoon dry white wine
1 tablespoon white wine vinegar
2 teaspoons dijon mustard
1½ tablespoons olive oil

1 Preheat the oven to 180°C (350°F/Gas 4). Halve the chickens by cutting down either side of the backbone. Discard the backbones. Cut the chickens into quarters, then brush with the oil and season lightly. Place on a rack in a roasting tin, skin side down, and roast for 20 minutes.

2 To make the honey glaze, combine the honey, lemon juice, zest, rosemary, wine, vinegar, mustard and oil in a small saucepan. Bring to the boil, then reduce the heat and simmer for about 5 minutes.

3 After cooking one side, turn the chickens over and baste well with the warm glaze. Return to the oven and roast for 20 minutes. Baste once more and cook for a further 15 minutes.

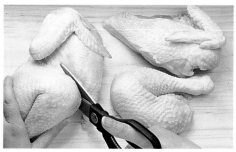

Cut the chicken into quarters, you will find kitchen scissors easier than a knife.

Cook one side of the chicken, then turn over and baste with the warm glaze.

NUTRITION PER SERVE (8)
Protein 70 g; Fat 10 g; Carbohydrate 8.5 g; Dietary
Fibre 0.5 g; Cholesterol 150 mg; 1693 kJ (405 Cal)

Creamy chicken, sage and tarragon pie

PREPARATION TIME: 25 MINUTES I TOTAL COOKING TIME: 1 HOUR 10 MINUTES I SERVES 4–6

1.5 kg (3 lb 5 oz) boneless, skinless
    chicken thighs
2 tablespoons olive oil
2 bacon slices, finely chopped
1 onion, roughly chopped
4 sage leaves, chopped
1 tablespoon chopped tarragon
45 g (1½ oz) butter, melted
2 tablespoons plain (all-purpose) flour
125 ml (4 fl oz/½ cup) milk
225 g (8 oz) tinned creamed corn
2 sheets ready-rolled puff pastry
1 egg, lightly beaten

1　Preheat the oven to 210°C (415°F/
Gas 6–7). Brush a 23 cm (9 inch) pie dish
with butter. Cut the chicken into bite-sized
pieces. Heat the oil in a large frying pan. Add
the chicken, bacon and onion, and cook over
medium heat for 5 minutes, or until browned.
Add the sage, tarragon, 250 ml (9 fl oz/1 cup)
water, salt and freshly ground pepper. Bring
to the boil, then reduce the heat and simmer,
covered, for 25 minutes, or until the chicken is
cooked through. Drain, reserving the juices.

2　Melt the butter in a heavy-based frying
pan. Add the flour and stir over low heat
for 1 minute. Remove from the heat and
gradually add the milk and reserved juice,
stirring until smooth. Return to the heat
and stir over medium heat until thickened.
Stir in the chicken mixture and corn. Spoon
into the pie dish.

3　Brush a sheet of pastry with egg and top
with a second sheet. Brush the rim of the pie
dish with egg and place the pastry over the
filling. Trim any excess.

4　Decorate the pie with pastry. Brush with egg
and make a few slits in the top. Bake for about
15 minutes, then reduce the heat to 180°C
(350°F/Gas 4) and bake for 10–15 minutes,
or until crisp and golden. Allow to slightly cool
for 5 minutes before cutting.

NUTRITION PER SERVE (6)
Protein 66 g; Fat 40 g; Carbohydrate 34 g; Dietary
Fibre 2.5 g; Cholesterol 217 mg; 3150 kJ (753 Cal)

Add the tarragon and sage, salt and pepper and
water to the chicken mixture.

Add the chicken mixture and corn to the sauce, and
stir to combine.

Chicken and watercress strudel

PREPARATION TIME: 30 MINUTES | TOTAL COOKING TIME: 50 MINUTES | SERVES 6

60 g (2¼ oz/¾ cup) fresh white breadcrumbs
1–2 teaspoons sesame seeds
60 g (2¼ oz/1 bunch) watercress, picked over
4 boneless, skinless chicken breasts
25 g (1 oz) butter
3 tablespoons dijon mustard
250 ml (9 fl oz/1 cup) thick (double/heavy) cream
15 sheets filo pastry
100 g (3½ oz) butter, melted

1 Preheat the oven to 190°C (375°F/Gas 5) and bake the breadcrumbs and sesame seeds, on separate trays, until golden. Steam the watercress for 3–5 minutes, or until just wilted, and squeeze out any water.

2 Slice the chicken into thin strips. Heat the butter in a frying pan and stir-fry the chicken until just cooked. Remove from the pan and season to taste. Stir the mustard and cream into the pan and simmer gently until reduced to about 125 ml (4 fl oz/½ cup). Remove from the heat and stir in the chicken and watercress.

3 Brush a sheet of filo pastry with melted butter and sprinkle with toasted breadcrumbs. Lay another filo sheet on top, brush with butter and sprinkle with breadcrumbs. Repeat with the remaining filo and breadcrumbs and place on a baking tray.

4 Place the chicken filling along the centre of the filo pastry. Fold the sides over and roll into a parcel, with the join underneath. Brush with the remaining butter and sprinkle with the toasted sesame seeds. Bake for 30 minutes, or until golden. Cool slightly before serving.

Steam the watercress until just wilted, then drain and squeeze out the water.

Fold the pastry sides to enclose the filling, then roll up into a parcel.

NUTRITION PER SERVE
Protein 25 g; Fat 65 g; Carbohydrate 30 g; Dietary Fibre 2 g; Cholesterol 235 mg; 3350 kJ (795 Cal)

Chicken pot pies with herb scones

PREPARATION TIME: 25 MINUTES | TOTAL COOKING TIME: 35 MINUTES | SERVES 6

60 g (2¼ oz/¼ cup) butter, melted, plus extra
    for greasing
1 onion, chopped
40 g (1½ oz/⅓ cup) plain (all-purpose) flour
670 ml (23 fl oz/2⅔ cups) milk
125 g (4½ oz/1 cup) grated cheddar cheese
2 teaspoons wholegrain mustard
450 g (1 lb/2½ cups) chopped cooked chicken
200 g (7 oz/2 cups) frozen mixed vegetables

TOPPING
250 g (9 oz/2 cups) self-raising flour
15 g (½ oz) butter
250 ml (9 fl oz/1 cup) milk
2 tablespoons chopped parsley
1 tablespoon milk, extra

1 Preheat the oven to 210°C (415°F/
Gas 6–7). Lightly grease six 250 ml (9 fl oz/
1 cup) individual dishes with butter. Heat the
butter in a large heavy-based frying pan. Add
the onion and cook over medium heat until soft.
Add the flour and stir for 1 minute, or until
lightly golden and bubbling. Gradually add the
milk, stirring constantly, until the sauce boils
and thickens. Remove from the heat. Stir in the
cheddar, mustard, chicken and vegetables. Spoon
the mixture evenly into the prepared dishes.

2 To make the topping, place the flour in a
bowl. Using your fingertips, rub the butter into
the flour, until the mixture is crumbly. Make a
well in the centre. Stir in the milk and parsley
with a flat-bladed knife. Using a cutting action,
stir until the mixture is soft and sticky.

3 On a floured surface, gather the dough into
a ball and roll to 2.5 cm (1 inch) thick. Cut into
rounds with a 4.5 cm (1¾ inch) cutter. Re-roll
the pastry scraps to cut more rounds. Place three
rounds on top of each chicken pot. Brush the
tops with milk. Bake for 25 minutes, until the
scones are cooked and the pies heated through.

NUTRITION PER SERVE
Protein 17 g; Fat 30 g; Carbohydrate 14 g; Dietary
Fibre 0.5 g; Cholesterol 95 mg; 1656 kJ (396 Cal)

Stir the cheese, mustard, chicken and vegetables
into the milk mixture.

Place three scone rounds on top of each of the
chicken pots.

Curried chicken pie

PREPARATION TIME: 45 MINUTES + 25 MINUTES REFRIGERATION | TOTAL COOKING TIME: 1 HOUR | SERVES 6

PASTRY
250 g (9 oz/2 cups) plain (all-purpose) flour
1 teaspoon ground turmeric
1 teaspoon ground cumin
125 g (4½ oz/½ cup) butter, cubed
1 egg, lightly beaten

1 cooked chicken (barbecued or poached)
40 g (1½ oz) butter, extra
1 onion, chopped
2 tablespoons curry powder
1 teaspoon cumin seeds
1 tablespoon plain (all-purpose) flour
375 ml (13 fl oz/1½ cups) chicken stock
125 ml (4 fl oz/½ cup) cream
1 tablespoon mango chutney
200 g (7 oz) sweet potato, cubed and cooked
milk, for glazing

1 To make the pastry, place the flour, turmeric, cumin and butter in a food processor. Process the mixture for about 15 seconds, or until crumbly. Add the egg and 2–3 tablespoons of cold water to bring the mixture together. Turn out onto a lightly floured surface and press together until smooth. Cover with plastic wrap and refrigerate for 20 minutes while making the filling.

2 Remove the skin and bones from the chicken and chop the meat into bite-sized pieces. Heat the butter in a deep frying pan and cook the onion until soft. Add the curry powder and cumin seeds and cook for about 1 minute longer.

3 Add the flour and cook for another 30 seconds. Remove from the heat and stir in the stock gradually, making sure the mixture is smooth between each addition. Return to the heat and cook, stirring, until the sauce bubbles and thickens. Add the cream, mango chutney, sweet potato and chicken. Simmer for 5 minutes, then season with salt and pepper. Remove from the heat and cool completely.

4 Preheat the oven to190°C (375°F/Gas 5). Divide the pastry into two portions. Roll out one half on a lightly floured surface until it is large enough to cover the base and side of a 23 cm (9 inch) pie dish. Line the dish with the pastry and spoon the chicken mixture into the base.

5 Roll out the remaining pastry to cover the top of the pie. Brush the adjoining edges with water, press together and trim the edges with a knife. Roll out the trimmings and cut into decorative shapes. Brush the base of the shapes with milk and press gently on to the pie.

6 Brush the top of the pie with milk and bake for 40 minutes, or until golden brown.

NUTRITION PER SERVE
Protein 30 g; Fat 50 g; Carbohydrate 40 g; Dietary Fibre 5 g; Cholesterol 240 mg; 2795 kJ (710 Cal)

Add the egg and enough cold water to bring the mixture together.

After removing the skin and bones, chop the chicken meat into bite-sized pieces.

Spoon the chicken mixture into the pastry lined pie dish

Beggars' chicken

PREPARATION TIME: 40 MINUTES + 30 MINUTES REFRIGERATION | TOTAL COOKING TIME: 1 HOUR 35 MINUTES | SERVES 4

4 x 400 g (14 oz) baby chickens

2 tablespoons olive oil
1 tablespoon soy sauce
2 tablespoons orange juice
1 tablespoon soft brown sugar
750 g (1 lb 10 oz/6 cups) plain
   (all-purpose) flour
1 kg (2 lb 4 oz) cooking salt
4 thin strips orange zest
4 star anise

1 Remove the giblets and any large fat deposits from the chickens. Pat the chickens dry with paper towels. Place the chickens in a shallow, non-metallic dish. Whisk the oil, soy sauce, orange juice and sugar in a bowl until combined. Brush the mixture all over the chickens, inside and out. Cover and refrigerate for 30 minutes. Preheat the oven to 240°C (475°F/Gas 8).

2 Sift the flour into a large mixing bowl and add the salt. Make a well in the centre and add 600 ml (21 fl oz) water all at once. Mix water into the flour and salt gradually, using your hands to make a firm dough. Turn onto a floured surface and press the dough together until smooth.

3 Divide the dough into four portions. Roll each portion out large enough to cover one of the chickens. Place a strip of orange zest and a star anise into the cavity of each chicken. Wrap each chicken securely with a greased sheet of foil then place, breast-side down, in the centre of a sheet of dough.

4 Wrap the dough over the chickens to enclose. Press firmly, ensuring there are no gaps or openings. Place breast side up in a large, shallow baking dish. Bake for 1 hour 35 minutes, or until the casing is crisp and well browned. Crack the casing with a hammer or meat mallet and discard. Remove the chicken from the foil. Serve the chicken with baked vegetables and peas.

Place a strip of orange zest and star anise into the cavity of each chicken.

Wrap the dough over the chicken to enclose it fully, ensuring there are no gaps or openings.

NUTRITION PER SERVE
Protein 52 g; Fat 15 g; Carbohydrate 280 g; Dietary Fibre 14 g; Cholesterol 25 mg; 6205 kJ (1482 Cal)

Smoked five-spice chicken

PREPARATION TIME: 30 MINUTES + OVERNIGHT MARINATING | TOTAL COOKING TIME: 50 MINUTES | SERVES 6

1 x 1.7 kg (3 lb 12 oz) chicken
60 ml (2 fl oz/¼ cup) soy sauce
1 tablespoon finely grated ginger
2 pieces dried mandarin or tangerine peel
   (see NOTE page 111)
1 star anise
¼ teaspoon five-spice
45 g (1½ oz/¼ cup) soft brown sugar

1 Wash the chicken in cold water. Pat dry with paper towels. Discard any large deposits of fat from inside the chicken. Place the chicken in a large non-metallic bowl with the soy sauce and grated ginger. Cover and refrigerate for several hours or overnight, turning occasionally.

2 Place a small rack in the base of a saucepan large enough to hold the chicken. Add water to this level. Place the chicken on the rack and bring the water to the boil. Cover tightly, reduce the heat and steam for 15 minutes. Turn off the heat and allow to stand, covered, for another 15 minutes. Transfer the chicken to a bowl.

3 Wash the pan and line with three or four large pieces of aluminium foil. Pound the dried peel and star anise using a mortar and pestle or crush with a rolling pin until the pieces are the size of coarse breadcrumbs. Add the five-spice and sugar, and spread over the foil.

4 Replace the rack in the pan and place the chicken on it. Place the pan over medium heat and, when the spice mixture starts smoking, cover tightly. Reduce the heat to low and smoke the chicken for 20 minutes. Test for doneness by piercing the thigh with a skewer. The juices should run clear. Remove the chicken from the pan and allow to cool before jointing it or chopping it Chinese-style.

VARIATION: *If you wish to save on cooking time, try the same method using half chicken breasts. Six chicken breasts will take 7 minutes to steam; smoking will take 8 minutes each side.*

NUTRITION PER SERVE
Protein 46 g; Fat 4.5 g; Carbohydrate 10 g; Dietary Fibre 0 g; Cholesterol 100 mg; 1126 kJ (270 cal)

Pound the dried peel with the star anise using a mortar and pestle.

Line the pan with foil and add the combined peel, star anise, five-spice and sugar.

Spicy roast chicken

PREPARATION TIME: 30 MINUTES I TOTAL COOKING TIME: 1 HOUR 25 MINUTES I SERVES 6

3 small dried red chillies
1 teaspoon fennel seeds
1 teaspoon cumin seeds
1 teaspoon coriander seeds
⅛ teaspoon salt
1.5 kg (3 lb 5 oz) chicken
2 garlic cloves, crushed
1 tablespoon peanut oil
2 onions, chopped
250 g (9 oz) minced (ground) pork
80 g (2¾ oz/½ cup) peanuts, roasted and
    roughly chopped
60 ml (2 fl oz/¼ cup) lime juice
1 tablespoon chopped mint
2 tablespoons chopped coriander (cilantro)
    leaves
1 teaspoon oil, extra
125 ml (4 fl oz/½ cup) coconut milk

NUTRITION PER SERVE
Protein 52 g; Fat 20 g; Carbohydrate 5 g; Dietary
Fibre 2 g; Cholesterol 105 mg; 1695 kJ (405 Cal)

1   Preheat the oven to 180°C (350°F/
Gas 4). Place the chillies, seeds and salt in
a small food processor or use a mortar and
pestle and process or grind until the spices
are blended to a powder.

2   Remove any fat from the chicken and rub
the skin and cavity with the garlic.

3   Heat the oil in a wok and cook the onion
over medium heat for 3 minutes, or until
golden. Add the pork and cook for 10 minutes,
or until brown. Remove from the heat, stir in
the peanuts, lime juice, mint and coriander.
Allow the mixture to cool slightly before
stuffing the chicken. Tightly secure the opening
with a wooden skewer, tie the legs together and
tuck the wing tips under.

4   Brush the chicken lightly with oil and then
rub the skin with the spice mixture. Place the
chicken on a rack in a baking dish and bake for
30 minutes. Remove from the oven and baste
with the coconut milk and pan juices. Bake
for 40 minutes, basting frequently, or until the
chicken is tender and the juices are running
clear when the thigh is pierced with a skewer.
Stand for 5 minutes. Remove the skewer and
string bevore carving. Serve with the stuffing.

Grind the chillies, fennel, cumin and coriander seeds and salt until they form a powder.

Spoon the prepared cooled stuffing into the cavity of the chicken.

Rub the spice mixture all over the surface of the chicken, using your fingers.

Ayam panggang

PREPARATION TIME: 20 MINUTES | TOTAL COOKING TIME: 1 HOUR | SERVES 4–6

1.5 kg (3 lb 5 oz) chicken
3 teaspoons chopped red and green chilli
3 garlic cloves, peeled
2 teaspoons dried green peppercorns, crushed
2 teaspoons soft brown sugar
2 tablespoons soy sauce
2 teaspoons ground turmeric
1 tablespoon lime juice
30 g (1 oz) butter, chopped

1 Preheat the oven to 180°C (350°F/Gas 4). Using a large cleaver, cut the chicken in half by cutting down the backbone and along the breastbone. Tuck the wing tips underneath the chicken to prevent them from burning. Place the chicken, skin side up, on a rack in a baking dish and bake for 30 minutes.

2 Meanwhile, combine the chilli, garlic, peppercorns and sugar in a small food processor or use a mortar and pestle and process briefly, or pound, until smooth. Add the soy sauce, turmeric and lime juice, and process in short bursts until combined.

3 Brush the spice mixture all over the chicken, dot with the butter pieces and bake for another 25–30 minutes, or until the juices run clear when the thigh is pierced with a skewer. Serve warm or at room temperature, garnished with lime wedges and fresh herbs.

Combine the chilli, garlic, peppercorns and brown sugar in a food processor.

Brush the spice mixture all over the chicken and bake until cooked through.

NUTRITION PER SERVE (6)
Protein 38 g; Fat 8 g; Carbohydrate 1.5 g; Dietary Fibre 0 g; Cholesterol 95 mg; 970 kJ (232 Cal)

Spicy spatchcocked chicken

PREPARATION TIME: 15 MINUTES + 4 HOURS MARINATING | TOTAL COOKING TIME: 20 MINUTES | SERVES 4

2 small chickens (750 g/1lb 10 oz each) or
   1 kg (2 lb 4 oz) chicken drumsticks
2 tablespoons malt vinegar or lemon juice
1½ teaspoons chilli powder
1½ teaspoons ground sweet paprika
2 teaspoons ground coriander
2 teaspoons ground cumin
1 teaspoon garam masala
1 tablespoon finely grated fresh ginger
1 tablespoon crushed garlic
80 g (2¾ oz) plain yoghurt
3 tablespoons ghee, melted, or oil

1   Pat the chickens dry with paper towels. Combine the vinegar, chilli, paprika, coriander, cumin, garam masala, ginger, garlic, salt and yoghurt in a large non-metallic bowl.

2   Using scissors, remove the backbones from the chickens. Turn the chickens over and flatten. Make several slashes in the skin. Place the chickens on a tray and coat well with the marinade, working it well into the flesh. Cover and refrigerate for 4 hours.

3   Place the chickens on a cold, lightly oiled grill. Brush with the melted ghee. Cook the chickens under a moderately hot grill for 20 minutes, or until cooked through, turning halfway through cooking and brushing occasionally with any remaining marinade. Serve the chickens with breads such as naan or chapatis, and lemon wedges.

VARIATION: *Grilling produces a good flavours, but for a delicious, smoky taste, prepare and marinate the chicken in the same way, then cook on a barbecue.*

HINT: *If you remove the chicken skin, the flavours of the marinade spices are able to penetrate the flesh much more effectively. Also, the finished dish will contain far less fat than if the skin were left on.*

NUTRITION PER SERVE
Protein 72 g; Fat 20 g; Carbohydrate 1.5 g; Dietary Fibre 0 g; Cholesterol 196 mg; 2009 kJ (480 Cal)

Mix the vinegar, chilli, paprika, coriander, cumin, garam masala, ginger, garlic, salt and yoghurt.

Using a pair of poultry scissors, remove the backbones from the chickens.

Chicken and leek pie

PREPARATION TIME: 20 MINUTES | TOTAL COOKING TIME: 40 MINUTES | SERVES 4

50 g (1¾ oz) butter
2 large leeks, washed and thinly sliced
4 spring onions (scallions), sliced
1 garlic clove, crushed
30 g (1 oz/¼ cup) plain (all-purpose) flour
375 ml (13 fl oz/1½ cups) chicken stock
125 ml (4 fl oz/½ cup) cream
1 medium barbecued chicken, chopped
2 sheets puff pastry, thawed
60 ml (2 fl oz/¼ cup) milk

1 Preheat the oven to 200°C (400°F/ Gas 6). In a frying pan, melt the butter and add the leek, spring onion and garlic. Cook over low heat for 6 minutes, or until the leek is soft but not browned. Sprinkle in the flour and mix well. Pour in the stock gradually and cook, stirring well, until the mixture is thick and smooth.

2 Stir in the cream and the chicken. Put the mixture in a shallow 20 cm (8 inch) pie dish and set aside to cool.

3 Cut a circle out of one of the sheets of pastry to cover the top of the pie. Brush around the rim of the pie dish with a little milk. Put the pastry on top and seal around the edge firmly. Trim off any overhanging pastry and decorate the edge with the back of a fork. Cut the other sheet into 1 cm (½ inch) strips and roll each strip up loosely into a spiral. Arrange the spirals on top of the pie, starting from the middle and leaving a gap between each one. The spirals may not cover the whole surface of the pie. Make a few small holes between the spirals to let out any steam, and brush the top of the pie lightly with milk. Bake for 25–30 minutes, or until the top is brown and crispy. Make sure the spirals look well cooked and are not raw in the middle.

NUTRITION PER SERVE
Protein 25 g; Fat 55 g; Carbohydrate 40 g; Dietary Fibre 3 g; Cholesterol 185 mg; 3105 kJ (740 Cal)

NOTE: *Make small pies by placing the mixture into 4 greased 310 ml (10¾ fl oz/1¼ cups) round ovenproof dishes. Cut the pastry into 4 rounds to fit. Bake for 15 minutes, or until crisp.*

Seal the edge firmly and trim off any overhanging pastry with a sharp knife.

Roll up the strips of pastry into spirals and arrange them on top of the pie.

Chicken and bacon gougère

PREPARATION TIME: 40 MINUTES | TOTAL COOKING TIME: 50 MINUTES | SERVES 6

60 g (2¼ oz/¼ cup) butter
1–2 garlic cloves, crushed
1 red onion, chopped
3 bacon slices, chopped
30 g (1 oz/¼ cup) plain (all-purpose) flour
375 ml (13 fl oz/1½ cups) milk
125 ml (4 fl oz/½ cup) cream
2 teaspoons wholegrain mustard
250 g (9 oz) cooked chicken, chopped
1 handful chopped parsley
1 tablespoon grated parmesan cheese

CHOUX PASTRY

60 g (2¼ oz/¼ cup) butter, chopped
60 g (2¼ oz/½ cup) plain (all-purpose) flour
2 eggs, lightly beaten
35 g (1¼ oz/⅓ cup) grated parmesan cheese

1 Melt the butter in a frying pan and cook the garlic, onion and bacon for 5–7 minutes, stirring occasionally, until soft but not browned. Stir in the flour and cook for 1 minute. Gradually add the milk and stir until thickened. Simmer for 2 minutes, then add the cream and mustard. Remove from the heat and fold in the chopped chicken and parsley. Season with pepper.

2 To make the pastry, place the butter and 125 ml (4 fl oz/½ cup) water in a saucepan. Stir until melted. Bring to the boil. Add the flour and beat for 2 minutes, or until the mixture leaves the side of the pan. Cool for 5 minutes. Gradually mix in the egg with an electric beater, until thick and glossy. Add the parmesan cheese.

3 Preheat the oven to 210°C (415°F/ Gas 6–7). Grease a deep 23 cm (9 inch) ovenproof dish, pour in the filling and spoon heaped tablespoons of choux pastry around the outside. Bake for 10 minutes, then reduce the oven to 180°C (350°F/ Gas 4) and bake for 20 minutes, or until the pastry is puffed and golden. Sprinkle with parmesan cheese.

Stir the garlic, onion and bacon until cooked but not browned.

Beat the pastry with a wooden spoon until the choux pastry leaves the sides of the pan.

NUTRITION PER SERVE
Protein 25 g; Fat 35 g; Carbohydrate 15 g; Dietary Fibre 1 g; Cholesterol 215 mg; 2010 kJ (480 Cal)

Chicken with figs and lemon

PREPARATION TIME: 20 MINUTES | TOTAL COOKING TIME: 35 MINUTES | SERVES 4

4 large chicken thigh cutlets
1 lemon
½ teaspoon ground ginger
½ teaspoon garam masala
1 tablespoon soy sauce
2 tablespoons olive oil
125 ml (4 fl oz/½ cup) sweet white wine
1 tablespoon ginger wine
60 ml (2 fl oz/¼ cup) lemon juice
2 chicken stock (bouillon) cubes, crumbled
6 plump dried figs, halved
2 teaspoons thinly sliced glacé (candied) ginger

1   Trim the chicken of fat and sinew. Preheat the oven to 180°C (350°F/Gas 4). Remove the lemon zest with a vegetable peeler and slice the zest into long thin strips. Place the zest in a small saucepan with a little water. Boil for 2 minutes, then drain and set aside.

2   Combine the ginger, garam masala and soy sauce. Rub the mixture all over the chicken.

3   Heat the oil in a heavy-based frying pan. Cook the chicken over medium heat for about 5 minutes on each side, or until well browned but not cooked through. Drain the chicken on paper towels. Transfer to a shallow ovenproof roasting tin.

4   Add the white wine, ginger wine, lemon juice, stock cubes and any remaining marinade to the same frying pan. Bring to the boil. Add the figs and glacé ginger. Remove from the heat and spoon over the chicken. Bake for 20 minutes, or until the chicken is tender, turning once. Serve with the lemon zest.

Remove the zest from the lemon and cut it into long thin strips.

Add the fig halves and glacé ginger to the boiling wine mixture.

NUTRITION PER SERVE
Protein 20 g; Fat 12 g; Carbohydrate 7 g; Dietary Fibre 2 g; Cholesterol 44 mg; 1018 kJ (245 cal)

Stews and casseroles

Clay-pot chicken and vegetables

PREPARATION TIME: 20 MINUTES + 30 MINUTES MARINATING | TOTAL COOKING TIME: 25 MINUTES | SERVES 4

500 g (1 lb 2 oz) boneless, skinless
    chicken thighs
1 tablespoon soy sauce
1 tablespoon dry sherry
6 dried Chinese mushrooms
2 small leeks
250 g (9 oz) orange sweet potato
2 tablespoons peanut oil
5 cm (2 inch) piece ginger, shredded
125 ml (4 fl oz/½ cup) chicken stock
1 teaspoon sesame oil
3 teaspoons cornflour (cornstarch)

1 Pat the chicken dry with paper towels. Cut into small pieces. Place in a dish with the soy sauce and sherry, cover and marinate for 30 minutes in the refrigerator.

2 Cover the mushrooms in hot water to soak for 30 minutes. Drain and squeeze to remove the excess liquid. Remove the stems and shred the caps.

3 Wash the leeks thoroughly to remove all the grit, then cut into thin slices. Cut the sweet potato into thin slices.

4 Drain the chicken, reserving the marinade. Heat half the peanut oil in a wok or heavy-based frying pan, swirling it gently to coat the base and side. Carefully add half the chicken pieces and stir-fry briefly until seared on all sides. Transfer to a flameproof clay pot or casserole. Stir-fry the remaining chicken and add to the clay pot.

5 Heat the remaining oil in the wok, add the leek and ginger and stir-fry for 1 minute. Add the mushrooms, the remaining marinade, the stock and sesame oil. Transfer to the clay pot, add the sweet potato and cook, covered, on the stovetop over very low heat for about 20 minutes. Dissolve the cornflour with a little water and add to the pot. Cook, stirring, until the mixture boils and thickens. Put chicken and vegetables in a serving dish and serve with steamed rice.

NUTRITION PER SERVE
Protein 30 g; Fat 15 g; Carbohydrate 13 g; Dietary
Fibre 2.5 g; Cholesterol 60 mg; 1277 kJ (305 Cal)

Wash the leeks thoroughly to remove all the grit, then cut into thin slices.

Stir-fry the marinated chicken pieces until seared on all sides.

Add the mushrooms, marinade, stock and sesame oil to the leek mixture.

Chicken adobo

PREPARATION TIME: 20 MINUTES + 2 HOURS MARINATING | TOTAL COOKING TIME: 1 HOUR | SERVES 6

1.5 kg (3 lb 5 oz) chicken pieces
6 garlic cloves, crushed
250 ml (9 fl oz/1 cup) cider vinegar
375 ml (13 fl oz/1½ cups) chicken stock
1 bay leaf
1 teaspoon coriander seeds
1 teaspoon black peppercorns
60 ml (2 fl oz/¼ cup) soy sauce
1 teaspoon annatto seeds or ¼ teaspoon
    paprika and ⅛ teaspoon turmeric
2 tablespoons oil

1 Combine all the ingredients, except the oil, in a large non-metallic bowl. Cover and refrigerate for 2 hours. Transfer the mixture to a large heavy-based frying pan and bring to the boil over high heat. Reduce the heat and simmer, covered, for 30 minutes. Uncover the pan and continue cooking for 10 minutes, or until the chicken is tender. Remove the chicken from the pan and set aside. Bring the liquid back to the boil and cook over high heat for 10 minutes, or until reduced by half.

2 Heat the oil in a wok or large non-stick frying pan and add the chicken in batches, cooking over medium heat for 5 minutes, or until crisp and golden. Serve the reduced sauce mixture over the chicken pieces and accompany with rice.

NUTRITION PER SERVE
Protein 38 g; Fat 10 g; Carbohydrate 0.5 g; Dietary Fibre 0.5 g; Cholesterol 83 mg; 1070 kJ (256 Cal)

Mix the chicken with the marinade and refrigerate, covered for 2 hours.

After removing the chicken from the pan, boil the liquid until it has reduced by half.

Cook the chicken pieces, in batches, until they are crisp and golden.

Braised chicken with chickpeas

PREPARATION TIME: 35 MINUTES | TOTAL COOKING TIME: 1 HOUR 35 MINUTES | SERVES 4

50 g (1¾ oz) butter

1 onion, roughly chopped

3 garlic cloves, crushed

1 carrot, finely chopped

½ celery stalk, finely chopped

1.5 kg (3 lb 5 oz) chicken pieces
(about 8 portions)

80 ml (2½ fl oz/⅓ cup) dry Marsala

250 ml (9 fl oz/1 cup) chicken stock

2 tablespoons lemon juice

40 g (1½ oz/½ cup) fresh breadcrumbs

300 g (10½ oz) tinned chickpeas, drained
and rinsed

200 g (7 oz) button mushrooms, sliced

2 tablespoons shredded mint

2 tablespoons chopped flat-leaf (Italian)
parsley

1 Heat half the butter in a large, heavy-based saucepan and cook the onion over medium heat until soft and golden. Add the garlic, carrot and celery and cook over gentle heat for 5 minutes. Remove from the pan and set aside.

2 Melt the remaining butter in the pan and brown the chicken in batches over high heat. Return all the chicken to the pan with the carrot and celery mixture. Quickly add the Marsala and stir well, scraping the sides and base of the pan. Add the stock and lemon juice, and bring to the boil. Reduce the heat and simmer gently for 1 hour, stirring occasionally.

3 Remove the chicken; keep warm. In a food processor, purée the contents of the pan, then add the breadcrumbs and blend for another 15 seconds.

4 Return the chicken to the pan, pour in the purée, add the chickpeas and mushrooms and simmer, covered, for 15 minutes. Season to taste, and scatter with mint and parsley to serve.

NUTRITION PER SERVE
Protein 120 g; Fat 30 g; Carbohydrate 50 g; Dietary
Fibre 15 g; Cholesterol 260 mg; 3900 kJ (930 Cal)

Pour the Marsala over the vegetables and chicken, stirring well.

Add the fresh breadcrumbs to the puréed vegetable mixture and process until smooth.

Chicken and orange casserole

PREPARATION TIME: 50 MINUTES | TOTAL COOKING TIME: 1 HOUR 40 MINUTES | SERVES 4–6

2 small chickens
1 tablespoon olive oil
2 thick bacon slices, rind removed and
  thinly sliced
50 g (1¾ oz) butter
16 baby onions, peeled, ends left intact
2–3 garlic cloves, crushed
3 teaspoons grated fresh ginger
2 teaspoons grated orange zest
2 teaspoons ground cumin
2 teaspoons ground coriander
2 tablespoons honey
250 ml (9 fl oz/1 cup) fresh orange juice
250 ml (9 fl oz/1 cup) dry white wine
125 ml (4 fl oz/½ cup) chicken or
  vegetable stock
350 g baby carrots
1 large parsnip, peeled

NUTRITION PER SERVE (6)
Protein 42 g; Fat 12 g; Carbohydrate 22 g; Dietary
Fibre 2 g; Cholesterol 135 mg; 1635 kJ (395 cal)

1 Using a pair of kitchen scissors, cut each chicken into 8 pieces, discarding the backbone. Remove any excess fat and discard (remove the skin as well, if preferred).

2 Heat about a teaspoon of the oil in a large, deep, heavy-based saucepan. Add the bacon and cook over medium heat for 2–3 minutes or until just crisp. Remove from the pan and drain on paper towels. Add the remaining oil and half the butter to the pan. Cook the onions, stirring occasionally, until dark golden brown. Remove from the pan and set aside. Add the chicken pieces to the pan and brown in small batches over medium heat. Remove from the pan, drain on paper towels.

3 Add the remaining butter to the pan. Stir in the garlic, ginger, orange zest, cumin, coriander and honey, and cook, stirring, for 1 minute. Add the orange juice, wine and stock to the pan. Bring to the boil, then reduce the heat and simmer for 1 minute. Return the chicken pieces to the pan, cover and leave to simmer over low heat for 40 minutes. Return the onions and bacon to the pan and simmer, covered, for a further 15 minutes. Remove the lid and leave to simmer for a further 15 minutes.

4 Trim the carrots, leaving a little green stalk, and wash well or peel, if necessary. Cut the parsnip into small batons. Add the carrots and parsnip to the pan. Cover and cook for about 5–10 minutes, or until the carrots and parsnip are just tender. To serve, put 2–3 chicken pieces on each plate, arrange the vegetables around it and spoon a little sauce over the top.

Cut each chicken into 8 pieces using a pair of kitchen scissors.

Add the orange juice, white wine and stock to the pan, and bring to the boil.

Return the browned baby onions and cooked bacon to the pan.

Creamy chicken with mushrooms

PREPARATION TIME: 20 MINUTES I TOTAL COOKING TIME: 50 MINUTES I SERVES 6

2 tablespoons olive oil
200 g (7 oz) button mushrooms, halved
200 g (7 oz) field mushrooms, chopped
1 small red capsicum (pepper), sliced
4 boneless, skinless chicken breasts, cut into
    bite-sized pieces
2 tablespoons plain (all-purpose) flour
250 ml (9 fl oz/1 cup) chicken stock
125 ml (4 fl oz/½ cup) red wine
3 spring onions (scallions), finely chopped
310 ml (10¾ fl oz/1¼ cups) cream
1 tablespoon chopped chives
1 tablespoon chopped flat-leaf (Italian)
    parsley, extra, to garnish
¼ teaspoon turmeric

1   Heat the oil in a large heavy-based saucepan
and add the button and field mushrooms and
capsicum. Cook over medium heat for 4 minutes,
or until soft. Remove and set aside.

2   Add the chicken to the pan in batches and
brown quickly over medium–high heat. Sprinkle
with the flour and cook for a further 2 minutes,
or until the flour is golden. Add the stock and
wine and bring to the boil. Cover and simmer
for 10 minutes, or until the chicken is tender.

3   Add the spring onion and cream, return to
the boil and simmer for 10–15 minutes, or until
the cream has reduced and thickened. Return
the mushrooms and capsicum to the pan and
add the chives, parsley and turmeric. Stir, season
to taste and simmer for a further 5 minutes to
heat through. Sprinkle with chopped parsley, just
before serving.

Choose large field mushrooms and wipe them with
a damp tea towel (dish towel) before chopping.

Add the mushrooms, capsicum, chives, parsley and
turmeric to the pan.

NUTRITION PER SERVE
Protein 40 g; Fat 33 g; Carbohydrate 6.5 g; Dietary
Fibre 2 g; Cholesterol 150 mg; 2060 kJ (493 Cal)

Apricot chicken

PREPARATION TIME: 10 MINUTES | TOTAL COOKING TIME: 1 HOUR | SERVES 6

6 chicken thigh cutlets

425 ml (15 fl oz) apricot nectar

40 g (1½ oz) packet French onion soup mix

425 g (15 oz) tinned apricot halves in natural juice, drained

60 g (2¼ oz/¼ cup) sour cream

1   Preheat the oven to 180°C (350°F/Gas 4). Remove the skin from the chicken thigh cutlets. Put the chicken in an ovenproof dish. Mix the apricot nectar with the French onion soup mix until well combined, and pour over the chicken.

2   Bake, covered, for 50 minutes, then add the apricot halves and bake for a further 5 minutes. Stir in the sour cream just before serving. Delicious served with creamy mashed potato or rice to soak up the juices.

NOTE: *If you are looking for a healthy alternative, you can use low-fat sour cream in place of the full-fat version.*

Pour in the apricot nectar and stir to combine with the soup mix.

Add the apricot halves to the chicken and bake for further 5 minutes.

NUTRITION PER SERVE
Protein 23 g; Fat 6 g; Carbohydrate 10 g; Dietary Fibre 0 g; Cholesterol 63 mg; 780 kJ (187 Cal)

Mediterranean chicken

PREPARATION TIME: 30 MINUTES I TOTAL COOKING TIME: 1 HOUR 10 MINUTES I SERVES 4

8 chicken thigh cutlets

2 tablespoons olive oil

150 g (5½ oz) French shallots (eschalots)

4 garlic cloves

125 ml (4 fl oz/½ cup) white wine

425 g (15 oz) tinned chopped tomatoes

12 Kalamata olives

1 tablespoon red wine vinegar

2 teaspoons tomato paste (concentrated purée)

1 tablespoon oregano

1 tablespoon chopped basil

1 teaspoon sugar

4 slices prosciutto

1 teaspoon grated lemon zest

1 handful chopped flat-leaf (Italian) parsley

1 tablespoon capers, rinsed

NUTRITION PER SERVE
Protein 75 g; Fat 25 g; Carbohydrate 15 g; Dietary
Fibre 8 g; Cholesterol 155 mg; 2390 kJ (570 Cal)

1 Preheat the oven to 180°C (350°F/ Gas 4). Remove the skin and fat from the chicken thighs. Heat half the oil in a large frying pan and brown the chicken over high heat for 3–4 minutes on each side. Arrange the chicken in a large flameproof casserole dish.

2 Heat the remaining oil in the same pan. Add the French shallots and garlic and cook over medium heat for 4 minutes, or until soft but not brown. Add the wine and bring to the boil.

3 Add the tomatoes, olives, vinegar, tomato paste, oregano, basil and sugar. Season with salt and black pepper. Boil, stirring, for 2 minutes, then pour over the chicken and cover with a tight-fitting lid. Bake for 45 minutes, or until the chicken is tender.

4 Meanwhile, place the prosciutto in a single layer in a frying pan. Dry-fry for 3 minutes, or until crisp, turning once. Break into large chunks and set aside.

5 Arrange the chicken on a serving dish, cover and keep warm. Transfer the casserole to the stovetop and boil the pan juices for 5 minutes, or until thickened, stirring occasionally. Spoon the juices over the chicken and sprinkle with the lemon zest, parsley and capers. Top with the prosciutto.

Cook the shallots and garlic until soft, then add the white wine.

Place the prosciutto slices in a single layer in a dry frying pan and fry until crisp.

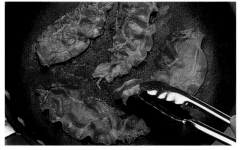

Persian chicken

PREPARATION TIME: 20 MINUTES | TOTAL COOKING TIME: 1 HOUR | SERVES 6

1.5 kg (3 lb 5 oz) chicken thighs
60 g (2¼ oz/½ cup) plain (all-purpose) flour
2 tablespoons olive oil
1 large onion, chopped
2 garlic cloves, chopped
½ teaspoon ground cinnamon
4 ripe tomatoes, chopped
6 fresh dates, stones removed, halved
2 tablespoons currants
500 ml (17 fl oz/2 cups) rich chicken stock
2 teaspoons finely grated lemon zest
80 g (2¾ oz/½ cup) almonds, toasted and
    roughly chopped
2 tablespoons chopped flat-leaf (Italian)
    parsley

1   Coat the chicken pieces with flour and shake off any excess. Heat the oil in a large heavy-based frying pan over medium heat. Brown the chicken on all sides, turning regularly, and then remove from the pan. Drain any excess oil from the pan.

2   Add the onion, garlic and ground cinnamon to the pan and cook, stirring regularly, for 5 minutes, or until the onion is soft.

3   Add the tomato, dates, currants and stock, and bring to the boil. Return the chicken to the pan, cover with the sauce, reduce the heat and simmer, uncovered, for 30 minutes. Add the lemon zest and season to taste. Bring back to the boil and boil for 5 minutes, or until thickened. Sprinkle with the almonds and parsley, and serve with buttered rice.

VARIATION: *Chicken drumsticks can be used instead of thighs.*

Coat the chicken pieces with the flour and shake off any excess.

Brown the chicken on all sides, turning regularly to prevent it from sticking.

NUTRITION PER SERVE
Protein 42 g; Fat 16 g; Carbohydrate 17 g; Dietary
Fibre 3.5 g; Cholesterol 83 mg; 1597 kJ (382 cal)

Spicy garlic chicken

PREPARATION TIME: 30 MINUTES | TOTAL COOKING TIME: 1 HOUR | SERVES 4–6

1.4 kg (3 lb 2 oz) chicken
1 handful coriander (cilantro) leaves with roots
2 tablespoons olive oil
4 garlic cloves, crushed
2 red onions, thinly sliced
1 large red capsicum (pepper), cut into squares
1 teaspoon ground ginger
1 teaspoon chilli powder
1 teaspoon caraway seeds, crushed
1 teaspoon ground turmeric
2 teaspoons ground coriander
2 teaspoons ground cumin
60 g (2¼ oz/½ cup) raisins
90 g (3¼ oz/½ cup) black olives
1 teaspoon finely grated lemon zest

1 Trim the chicken of excess fat and sinew. Cut the chicken into 12 serving pieces. Finely chop the coriander roots, reserving the leaves.

2 Heat the oil in a large heavy-based frying pan. Add the garlic, onion, capsicum, ginger, chilli powder, caraway seeds, turmeric, coriander, cumin and coriander roots. Cook over medium heat for 10 minutes.

3 Add the chicken pieces and stir until combined. Add 375 ml (13 fl oz/1½ cups) water and bring to the boil. Reduce the heat and simmer for 45 minutes, or until the chicken is tender and cooked through.

4 Add the raisins, black olives and lemon zest and simmer for a further 5 minutes. Serve with bread and green vegetables. May be served sprinkled with the reserved coriander leaves.

VARIATION: *Chicken pieces may be used instead of a whole chicken.*

NUTRITION PER SERVE (6)
Protein 33 g; Fat 13 g; Carbohydrate 13 g; Dietary Fibre 2 g; Cholesterol 105 mg; 1236 kJ (295 Cal)

Wash the coriander and finely chop the roots, reserving the leaves.

Add the raisins, olives and lemon zest to the chicken mixture.

Vietnamese chicken and noodle casserole

PREPARATION TIME: 40 MINUTES | TOTAL COOKING TIME: 30 MINUTES | SERVES 4

1 lemongrass stem, white part only
4 makrut (kaffir lime) leaves
1 litre (35 fl oz/4 cups) chicken stock
400 ml (14 fl oz) coconut cream
30 g (1 oz/¼ cup) coconut milk powder
2 tablespoons peanut oil
400 g (14 oz) chicken breasts, cut into strips
12 raw king prawns, peeled and deveined,
    tails intact
8 spring onions (scallions), sliced
2 teaspoons finely chopped fresh ginger
4 garlic cloves, finely chopped
2 small red chillies, seeded and
    finely chopped
500 g (1 lb 2 oz) hokkien (egg) noodles
1 teaspoon dried shrimp paste
2 tablespoons lime juice
90 g (3¼ oz/1 cup) bean sprouts
mint leaves, to garnish
coriander leaves, to garnish

1   Peel away outer leaves of the lemongrass stem to the first purple ring. Chop the white part of the lemongrass finely. Remove the centre stem from the makrut leaves, then finely shred the makrut.

2   Place the lemongrass and makrut in a large, heavy-based saucepan with the stock, coconut cream and coconut milk powder. Bring to the boil, stirring constantly to dissolve the coconut milk powder. Reduce the heat and simmer, covered, for 15 minutes.

3   Heat a wok over high heat and add the peanut oil. Add the chicken, prawns, spring onion, ginger, garlic and chilli. Stir-fry for 5–10 minutes, or until the chicken and prawns are cooked through.

4   Place the noodles in the simmering coconut cream, then add the chicken and prawn mixture from the wok. Add the shrimp paste and lime juice. Allow the noodles to heat through.

5   Divide the sprouts among warmed deep bowls and place the noodles, chicken and prawns on top. Ladle the sauce over, scatter with mint and coriander and serve at once.

NUTRITION PER SERVE
Protein 40 g; Fat 35 g; Carbohydrate 10 g; Dietary Fibre 4 g; Cholesterol 135 mg; 2150 kJ (515 Cal)

Using a sharp knife, finely chop the white stem of the lemongrass.

Stir-fry the chicken, prawns, spring onion, ginger, garlic and chilli.

Add the hokkien noodles to the simmering coconut cream mixture.

White-cooked chicken with spring onion sauce

PREPARATION TIME: 5 MINUTES | TOTAL COOKING TIME: 1 HOUR + 1 HOUR REFRIGERATION | SERVES 6

1.8 kg (4 lb) chicken
3 slices fresh ginger
1½ teaspoons salt
iced water (see HINT)

SPRING ONION SAUCE
2 tablespoons oil
3 spring onions (scallions), thinly sliced
1 tablespoon soy sauce

1 Remove any pockets of fat from the chicken, then remove and discard the tail. Place the chicken in a large saucepan and add enough water to cover. Add the ginger and salt and bring to the boil. Cover and simmer for 20 minutes.

2 Turn off the heat, keeping the pan covered tightly. Set aside for 35 minutes. Remove the chicken carefully from the pan, draining off any of the stock that has lodged inside. Plunge the chicken into a large bowl of iced water. This process stops the chicken cooking and tightens the skin, sealing in the juices.

3 Leave the cooled chicken in the bowl of iced water and chill in the refrigerator for 1 hour. Just before serving, drain the chicken from the water and chop, Chinese-style.

4 To make the spring onion sauce, heat the oil in a wok, add the spring onion and cook briefly just to heat through. Stir in the soy sauce. Serve the chicken in deep plates with the spring onion sauce poured over.

HINT: *Use this recipe whenever cold, boiled chicken is called for. Because the chicken never boils and is chilled very rapidly, the juices are sealed in and the result is very succulent, moist and tender. To achieve the result required, it is essential that the water into which the chicken is plunged is very well chilled. Add 2 or 3 trays of ice cubes to ensure that it is as cold as possible.*

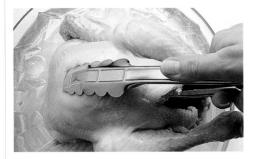

Plunge the chicken into a large bowl filled with iced water to stop the cooking process.

Just before serving, drain the chicken from the water and chop Chinese-style.

NUTRITION PER SERVE
Protein 50 g; Fat 11 g; Carbohydrate 0.5 g; Dietary Fibre 0 g; Cholesterol 110 mg; 1265 kJ (302 Cal)

Country-style chicken with baby vegetables

PREPARATION TIME: 45 MINUTES | TOTAL COOKING TIME: 2 HOURS | SERVES 4

1.5 kg (3 lb 5 oz) chicken pieces (about
    8 portions)
60 g (2¼ oz/¼ cup) clarified butter
12 baby onions
250 ml (9 fl oz/1 cup) dry white wine
250 ml (9 fl oz/1 cup) chicken stock
250 ml (9 fl oz/1 cup) cream
12 baby carrots
16 snow peas (mangetouts)
16 asparagus spears
12 button mushrooms
1 tablespoon snipped chives

1 Season the chicken portions with a little salt and pepper. Heat half the butter in a frying pan, then brown the chicken in batches for 2–3 minutes on each side to seal the flavours. Place in a casserole dish and add the onions. Preheat the oven to 200°C (400°F/Gas 6).

2 Pour the wine into the frying pan and stir over medium heat, scraping down the side and base of the pan. Add the stock and whisk in the cream. Bring to the boil, then reduce the heat and simmer for 20 minutes. Pour the sauce over the chicken. Cover and bake for 1 hour 10 minutes.

3 Meanwhile, bring a saucepan of salted water to the boil. In separate batches, boil or steam the carrots, snow peas and asparagus until just cooked, but still slightly crunchy. Plunge in iced water, then drain and set aside.

4 Heat the remaining butter in a frying pan. Sauté the mushrooms for 2–3 minutes, stirring constantly.

5 Place the mushrooms on top of the stew with the blanched vegetables and cook for another 20 minutes, or until the chicken is tender. Skim off any fat, stir carefully to mix all the vegetables through and sprinkle with the chives to serve.

NUTRITION PER SERVE
Protein 95 g; Fat 50 g; Carbohydrate 15 g; Dietary
Fibre 4 g; Cholesterol 350 mg; 4040 kJ (965 Cal)

Lightly brown the seasoned chicken in half the melted butter.

Plunge the blanched vegetables into a bowl of iced water to stop them from cooking.

Majorcan chicken

PREPARATION TIME: 30 MINUTES | TOTAL COOKING TIME: 1 HOUR 30 MINUTES | SERVES 4

2 tablespoons olive oil

30 g (1 oz) butter

1.5 kg (3 lb 5 oz) chicken pieces

1 orange

1 red onion, thinly sliced

2 garlic cloves, chopped

185 ml (6 fl oz/¾ cup) chicken stock

125 ml (4 fl oz/½ cup) dry white wine

1 tablespoon plain (all-purpose) flour

1 red capsicum (pepper), quartered

12 stuffed green olives

NUTRITION PER SERVE
Protein 90 g; Fat 25 g; Carbohydrate 10 g; Dietary
Fibre 4 g; Cholesterol 205 mg; 2700 kJ (645 Cal)

1   Preheat the oven to 180°C (350°F/Gas 4). Heat the oil and butter in a large frying pan. Brown the chicken in batches over high heat and transfer to a flameproof casserole dish.

2   Cut two large strips of zest from the orange and set aside. Remove the pith from the orange, then slice the orange into thin rounds. Set aside.

3   Cook the onion and garlic in the frying pan for 3 minutes over medium heat, or until softened. Combine the stock and wine. Stir the flour into the pan, then slowly add the stock and wine and stir until the mixture comes to the boil. Add the orange zest strips, then pour over the chicken. Cover and bake for 1 hour.

4   Meanwhile, grill the capsicum, skin side up, for 8 minutes, or until black and blistered. Place in a plastic bag, seal and allow to cool. Peel away the skin and cut the flesh into strips.

5   Remove the chicken from the dish; cover and keep warm. Bring the sauce to the boil on the stovetop, skimming off the fat. Boil for 5 minutes to thicken slightly. Add the capsicum strips, orange slices and olives. To serve, remove the orange zest, season to taste and spoon the sauce over the chicken.

Peel two strips of orange zest. Remove the pith and slice the orange into rounds.

Grill the capsicum, skin side up, until the skin is black and blistered.

Stir the capsicum strips, orange slices, olives and parsley into the sauce.

Chicken cacciatore

PREPARATION TIME: 45 MINUTES I TOTAL COOKING TIME: 1 HOUR 20 MINUTES I SERVES 4

4 tomatoes
1.5 kg (3 lb 5 oz) chicken pieces
20 g (¾ oz) butter
1 tablespoon oil
20 g (¾ oz) butter, extra
1 large onion, chopped
2 garlic cloves, chopped
1 small green capsicum (pepper), chopped
150 g (5½ oz) mushrooms, thickly sliced
1 tablespoon plain (all-purpose) flour
250 ml (9 fl oz/1 cup) dry white wine
1 tablespoon white wine vinegar
2 tablespoons tomato paste
    (concentrated purée)
90 g (3¼ oz/½ cup) small black olives
4 tablespoons chopped parsley

1 Score a cross in the base of each tomato. Put the tomatoes in a bowl of boiling water for 30 seconds, then transfer to a bowl of cold water. Drain, peel the skin away from the cross. Halve the tomatoes and remove the seeds. Chop the flesh. Preheat the oven to 180°C (350°F/Gas 4).

2 Remove excess fat from the chicken pieces and pat dry with paper towels. Heat half the butter and oil in a large flameproof casserole. Cook half the chicken over high heat until browned all over, then set aside. Heat the remaining butter and oil and cook the remaining chicken. Set aside.

3 Heat the extra butter in the casserole and cook the onion and garlic for 2–3 minutes. Add the capsicum and mushrooms, and cook, stirring, for 3 minutes. Stir in the flour and cook for 1 minute. Add the wine, vinegar, tomato and tomato paste and cook, stirring, for 2 minutes, or until slightly thickened. Return the chicken to the casserole and make sure it is covered by the tomato and onion mixture. Place in the oven and cook, covered, for 1 hour, or until the chicken is tender. Stir in the olives and parsley. Season and serve with pasta.

Drain the tomatoes, then peel away the skin from the cross.

Cut the tomatoes in half and remove the seeds with a teaspoon.

NUTRITION PER SERVE
Protein 55 g; Fat 15 g; Carbohydrate 9.5 g; Dietary Fibre 5 g; Cholesterol 125 mg; 1675 kJ (401 Cal)

Chicken paprika

PREPARATION TIME: 25 MINUTES | TOTAL COOKING TIME: 45 MINUTES | SERVES 4–6

800 g (1 lb 12 oz) boneless, skinless
    chicken thighs
60 g (2¼ oz/½ cup) plain (all-purpose) flour
2 tablespoons vegetable oil
2 onions, chopped
1–2 garlic cloves, crushed
2 tablespoons sweet paprika
125 ml (4½ fl oz/½ cup) good-quality dry
    red wine
1 tablespoon tomato paste
    (concentrated purée)
425 g (15 oz) tinned chopped tomatoes
200 g (7 oz) button mushrooms
125 ml (4 fl oz/½ cup) chicken stock
80 g (2¾ oz) sour cream

1   Rinse the chicken and dry well with paper towel. Trim the chicken of excess fat and sinew. Cut the chicken into 3 cm (1¼ inch) pieces. Season the flour with salt and pepper. Toss the chicken pieces lightly in the seasoned flour, shake off the excess and reserve the flour. Heat half the oil in a large heavy-based frying pan. Cook the chicken pieces quickly in small batches over medium–high heat. Remove from the pan and drain on paper towels.

2   Heat the remaining oil in the pan and add the onion and garlic. Cook, stirring, until the onion is soft. Add the paprika and reserved flour, and stir for 1 minute. Add the chicken, wine, tomato paste and undrained crushed tomato. Bring to the boil, then reduce the heat and simmer, covered, for 15 minutes.

3   Add the mushrooms and chicken stock. Simmer, covered, for a further 10 minutes. Add the sour cream and stir until heated through, but do not allow to boil.

NUTRITION PER SERVE (6)
Protein 35 g; Fat 20 g; Carbohydrate 14 g; Dietary
Fibre 3 g; Cholesterol 105 mg; 1668 kJ (399 Cal)

Trim the chicken thighs of excess fat and sinew, and cut into pieces.

Stir in the sour cream until heated through, but do not allow to boil.

Coq au vin

PREPARATION TIME: 20 MINUTES | TOTAL COOKING TIME: 1 HOUR | SERVES 6

2 thyme sprigs

4 parsley sprigs

2 bay leaves

2 kg (4 lb 8 oz) chicken pieces

plain (all-purpose) flour, seasoned with salt
    and freshly ground pepper

60 ml (2 fl oz/¼ cup) oil

4 thick bacon slices, sliced

12 baby onions

2 garlic cloves, crushed

2 tablespoons brandy

375 ml (13 fl oz/1½ cups) dry red wine

375 ml (13 fl oz/1½ cups) chicken stock

60 g (2¼ oz/¼ cup) tomato paste
    (concentrated purée)

250 g (9 oz) button mushrooms

1 Make a bouquet garni by wrapping the thyme, parsley and bay leaves in a small square of muslin and tying them well with string, or tying them between two 5 cm (2 inch) lengths of celery.

2 Toss the chicken in the seasoned flour to coat, shaking off any excess. In a heavy-based saucepan, heat 2 tablespoons of the oil and brown the chicken in batches over medium heat. Drain on paper towels.

3 Wipe the pan clean with paper towels and heat the remaining oil. Add the bacon, onions and garlic and cook, stirring, until the onions are browned. Add the chicken, brandy, wine, stock, bouquet garni and tomato paste. Bring to the boil, reduce the heat and simmer, covered, for 30 minutes.

4 Stir in the mushrooms and simmer, uncovered, for 10 minutes, or until the chicken is tender and the sauce has thickened. Remove the bouquet garni.

NOTE: *Don't be tempted to use poor-quality wine for cooking, as the taste will affect the flavour of the dish.*

NUTRITION PER SERVE
Protein 80 g; Fat 20 g; Carbohydrate 7 g; Dietary Fibre 2 g; Cholesterol 180 mg; 2420 kJ (580 Cal)

Wrap the thyme, parsley and bay leaves in a small square of muslin.

In batches, brown the chicken in the hot oil over medium heat.

Return the chicken to the pan with the liquids, bouquet garni and tomato paste.

Chicken mole

PREPARATION TIME: 25 MINUTES I TOTAL COOKING TIME: 1 HOUR 10 MINUTES I SERVES 4

8 chicken drumsticks
plain (all-purpose) flour, for dusting
cooking oil spray
1 large onion, finely chopped
2 garlic cloves, finely chopped
1 teaspoon ground cumin
1 teaspoon chilli powder
2 teaspoons cocoa powder
440 g (15½ oz) tinned tomatoes,
    roughly chopped
440 g (15½ fl oz) tomato paste
    (concentrated purée)
250 ml (9 fl oz/1 cup) chicken stock
toasted almonds, to garnish
chopped parsley, to garnish

1   Remove and discard the chicken skin. Wipe
the chicken with paper towels and lightly dust
with the flour. Spray a large, deep, non-stick
frying pan with oil. Cook the chicken for
8 minutes over high heat, turning until
golden brown. Remove and set aside.

2   Add the onion, garlic, cumin, chilli powder,
cocoa, 1 teaspoon salt, ½ teaspoon black pepper
and 60 ml (2 fl oz/¼ cup) water to the pan and
cook for 5 minutes, or until softened.

3   Stir in the tomato, tomato paste and chicken
stock. Bring to the boil, then add the chicken
drumsticks, cover and simmer for 45 minutes, or
until tender. Uncover and simmer for 5 minutes,
until the mixture is thick. Garnish with the
almonds and parsley.

NOTE: *This is a traditional Mexican dish, usually
flavoured with a special type of dark chocolate
rather than cocoa powder.*

Pull the skin off the chicken drumsticks, then wipe
the chicken with paper towels.

Stir in the onion, garlic, cumin, chilli powder,
cocoa, salt, pepper and water.

NUTRITION PER SERVE
Protein 25 g; Fat 7 g; Carbohydrate 10 g; Dietary
Fibre 4 g; Cholesterol 100 mg; 910 kJ (220 Cal)

Chicken chasseur

PREPARATION TIME: 20 MINUTES | TOTAL COOKING TIME: 1 HOUR 30 MINUTES | SERVES 4

1 kg (2 lb 4 oz) boneless, skinless chicken thighs

2 tablespoons olive oil

1 garlic clove, crushed

1 large onion, sliced

100 g (3½ oz) button mushrooms, sliced

1 teaspoon thyme leaves

400 g (14 oz) tinned chopped tomatoes

60 ml (2 fl oz/¼ cup) chicken stock

60 ml (2 fl oz/¼ cup) dry white wine

1 tablespoon tomato paste
(concentrated purée)

1   Preheat the oven to 180°C (350°F/Gas 4). Trim the chicken of excess fat and sinew. Heat the oil in a heavy-based frying pan and brown the chicken in batches over medium heat. Drain on paper towels, then transfer to a casserole dish.

2   Add the garlic, onion and sliced mushrooms to the pan and cook over medium heat for about 5 minutes, or until soft. Add to the chicken with the thyme and tomatoes.

3   Combine the stock, wine and tomato paste and pour over the chicken. Bake, covered, for 1¼ hours, or until the chicken is cooked through and tender.

NUTRITION PER SERVE
Protein 60 g; Fat 15 g; Carbohydrate 6 g; Dietary Fibre 2 g; Cholesterol 125 mg; 1710 kJ (410 Cal)

Brown the chicken in the hot oil over medium heat and drain on paper towels.

Add the garlic, onion and mushrooms to the pan and cook until soft.

Pour the combined stock, wine and tomato paste over the chicken mixture.

Chicken and mushroom casserole

PREPARATION TIME: 20 MINUTES | TOTAL COOKING TIME: 1 HOUR 10 MINUTES | SERVES 4

20 g (¾ oz) dried porcini mushrooms
30 g (1 oz/¼ cup) plain (all-purpose) flour
1.5 kg (3 lb 5 oz) chicken pieces
2 tablespoons vegetable oil
1 large onion, chopped
2 garlic cloves, crushed
60 ml (2 fl oz/¼ cup) chicken stock
80 ml (2½ fl oz/⅓ cup) dry white wine
425 g (15 oz) tinned peeled whole tomatoes
1 tablespoon balsamic vinegar
3 thyme sprigs
1 bay leaf
300 g (10½ oz) field mushrooms,
    thickly sliced

NUTRITION PER SERVE
Protein 55 g; Fat 10 g; Carbohydrate 7 g; Dietary
Fibre 4 g; Cholesterol 115 mg; 1515 kJ (360 Cal)

1   Preheat the oven to 180°C (350°F/Gas 4).
Put the porcini mushrooms in a bowl and
cover with 60 ml (2 fl oz/¼ cup) boiling water.
Leave for 5 minutes, or until the mushrooms
are rehydrated.

2   Season the flour with salt and freshly
ground pepper. Lightly toss the chicken in the
flour to coat and shake off any excess.

3   Heat the oil in a flameproof casserole and
cook the chicken in batches until well browned
all over. Set aside. Add the onion and garlic to
the casserole and cook for 3–5 minutes, or until
the onion softens. Stir in the stock.

4   Return the chicken to the casserole with the
porcini mushrooms and any remaining liquid,
wine, tomatoes, vinegar, thyme and bay leaf.
Cover and cook in the oven for 30 minutes.

5   After 30 minutes, remove the lid and add
the field mushrooms. Return to the oven and
cook, uncovered, for 15–20 minutes, or until
the sauce thickens slightly. Serve with boiled
potatoes and sprinkle with chopped parsley.

Cover the porcini mushrooms with boiling water and soak until rehydrated.

Lightly toss the chicken pieces in the flour and shake off any excess.

Add the chicken to the casserole and cook in batches until browned.

Creamy tomato and chicken stew

PREPARATION TIME: 35 MINUTES | TOTAL COOKING TIME: 50 MINUTES | SERVES 4–6

4 bacon slices

2 tablespoons vegetable oil

50 g (1¾ oz) butter

300 g (10½ oz) small button
mushrooms, halved

1.5 kg (3 lb 5 oz) chicken pieces

2 onions, chopped

2 garlic cloves, crushed

400 g (14 oz) tinned whole peeled tomatoes

250 ml (9 fl oz/1 cup) chicken stock

250 ml (9 fl oz/1 cup) cream

2 tablespoons chopped flat-leaf
(Italian) parsley

2 tablespoons lemon thyme leaves

NUTRITION PER SERVE (6)
Protein 70 g; Fat 40 g; Carbohydrate 7 g; Dietary
Fibre 3 g; Cholesterol 215 mg; 2650 kJ (630 Cal)

1   Chop the bacon into large pieces. Place a large, heavy-based saucepan over medium heat. Brown the bacon, then remove and set aside on paper towels.

2   Heat half the oil and a third of the butter in the pan until foaming, then stir in the mushrooms and cook until softened and golden brown. Remove from the saucepan with a slotted spoon.

3   Add the remaining oil to the pan with a little more butter. When the oil is hot, brown the chicken pieces in batches over high heat until the skin is golden all over and a little crisp. Remove from the pan.

4   Heat the remaining butter in the pan. Add the onion and garlic and cook over medium–high heat for about 3 minutes, or until softened. Pour in the tomato, stock and cream. Return the bacon, mushrooms and chicken pieces to the pan and simmer over medium–low heat for 25 minutes. Stir in the herbs, season with salt and freshly ground pepper and simmer for another 5 minutes before serving.

When the oil and butter are foaming, add the mushrooms and cook until soft.

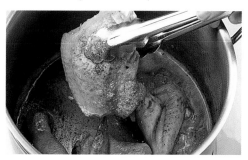
Brown the chicken pieces in batches over high heat until the skin is golden and crisp.

Add the tomatoes, stock and cream to the softened onion and garlic.

Spicy chicken and beans

PREPARATION TIME: 30 MINUTES | TOTAL COOKING TIME: 50 MINUTES | SERVES 4

1 tablespoon olive oil
4 spring onions (scallions), finely chopped
1 celery stalk, finely chopped
1 jalapeño chilli, seeded and chopped
500 g (1 lb 2 oz) minced (ground) chicken
3 garlic cloves, crushed
¼ teaspoon ground cinnamon
¼ teaspoon chilli powder
1 teaspoon ground cumin
2 teaspoons plain (all-purpose) flour
425 g (15 oz) tinned chopped tomatoes
125 ml (4 fl oz/½ cup) chicken stock
2 x 300 g (10½ oz) tinned butter
    beans, drained
2 teaspoons soft brown sugar
4 tablespoons finely chopped coriander
    (cilantro) leaves

1   Heat the oil in a large frying pan, add the spring onion and cook until softened. Add the celery and chilli and cook for 1–2 minutes. Increase the heat, add the mince and brown, breaking up lumps with a fork or wooden spoon. Stir in the garlic, cinnamon, chilli powder and cumin. Cook for 1 minute. Add the flour to the pan and stir well.

2   Stir in the tomato and stock. Bring the mixture to the boil, reduce the heat and simmer, covered, for 10–15 minutes.

3   Add the butter beans to the pan and simmer for another 15 minutes, or until the liquid is reduced to a thick sauce. Add the sugar and season, to taste. Just before serving, scatter the coriander over the top.

Add the minced chicken to the pan and stir until brown, breaking up any lumps.

Add the drained butter beans to the pan and simmer for another 15 minutes.

NUTRITION PER SERVE
Protein 35 g; Fat 8.5 g; Carbohydrate 12 g; Dietary Fibre 6.5 g; Cholesterol 63 mg; 1113 kJ (266 Cal)

Moroccan chicken

PREPARATION TIME: 20 MINUTES + 2 HOURS MARINATING I TOTAL COOKING TIME: 1 HOUR 25 MINUTES I SERVES 4

8 large chicken drumsticks
3 garlic cloves, crushed
1 teaspoon grated fresh ginger
1 teaspoon ground turmeric
2 teaspoons ground cumin
1 teaspoon ground cardamom
1 teaspoon finely grated lemon zest
2 tablespoons oil
1 onion, sliced
500 ml (17 fl oz/2 cups) chicken stock
6 pitted dates, chopped
20 g (¾ oz/⅓ cup) shredded coconut
1 tablespoon flat-leaf (Italian) parsley

1 Trim the chicken of excess fat and sinew. Place the chicken in a large non-metallic bowl. Combine the garlic, ginger, turmeric, cumin, cardamom and lemon zest in a small bowl. Add to the chicken and stir to completely coat. Cover and marinate for 2 hours.

2 Preheat the oven to 180°C (350°F/Gas 4). Heat the oil in a large heavy-based frying pan. Cook the chicken quickly over medium heat until well browned. Drain on paper towels. Place the chicken in an ovenproof casserole dish.

3 Add the onion to the pan and cook, stirring, for 5 minutes, or until soft. Add the cooked onion, stock, dates and shredded coconut to the casserole dish. Cover and bake for 1¼ hours, or until the chicken is tender, stirring occasionally.

NOTE: *The chicken may be left to marinate overnight in the refrigerator.*

VARIATION: *Dried apricots or prunes are great alternatives to dates.*

NUTRITION PER SERVE
Protein 47 g; Fat 18 g; Carbohydrate 9 g; Dietary Fibre 2.8 g; Cholesterol 100 mg; 1622 kJ (388 Cal)

Add the combined garlic, ginger, tumeric, cumin, cardamom and lemon zest to the chicken.

Add the onion, stock, dates and coconut to the casserole dish.

Basics

Chicken Basics

Fresh chicken

Fresh chicken has better flavour and texture than frozen. Look for skin that is light pink and moist, rather than wet, with no dry spots. The breast should be plump and well rounded; on a young bird the point of the breastbone will be flexible. At speciality poultry shops you can buy free-range, grain-fed, and corn-fed chickens (with yellow skin and flesh). Chicken can also be purchased cooked. Cooked, smoked chicken is available whole, chilled, from delicatessens and supermarkets.

Chicken cuts include: double or single breasts on the bone, with skin or without; breast fillets; tenderloins (the part just behind the breast); marylands (the whole thigh and leg); thigh cutlets; thigh fillets; wings; and drumsticks (the bottom part of the leg). Chicken is very versatile, and it is not always necessary to buy the most expensive fillets to produce an excellent result. Here is a guide to the cuts used in this book.

For roasting – whole roasting chickens, baby chickens, whole breasts, wings, leg quarters (marylands), drumsticks, thighs.
For grilling – chicken halves and quarters, wings, drumsticks, leg quarters (marylands), thigh cutlets. **For barbecuing** – chicken halves, whole breasts, wings, drumsticks, leg quarters (marylands), thigh cutlets, tenderloins.

For stir-frying – breast fillets, thigh fillets, tenderloins, livers.
For pan-frying – leg quarters (marylands), breast fillets, tenderloins, livers.
For deep-frying – drumsticks, wings, thighs, chicken pieces.
For casseroles/braising – whole chickens, chicken pieces, thighs, thigh cutlets, drumsticks, wings.
For poaching – whole chickens, whole breasts, breast fillets, thighs, drumsticks.
For stock – bones, necks, giblets, boiling fowls.

Storing fresh chicken: Chicken must be transported home as quickly as possible. Do not leave it sitting in the sun in the car or car boot. The internal temperature of a car left closed in full sun spells disaster to all chicken products. The longer that food spends between 5°C (41°F) and 60°C (140°F), the greater the likelihood of rapid growth of harmful bacteria that may result in food poisoning. Keep chicken away from any strong-smelling items such as cleaning agents and petrol that you may have stored in your vehicle; chicken will absorb the smells. In hot weather, use an insulated chiller bag to keep it cold. It is particularly important to store poultry carefully to avoid contamination by salmonella bacteria, which can cause food poisoning. Always wash hands, chopping boards, knives and cooking implements in very hot soapy water after handling raw chicken.

Always keep cooked and raw chicken separate. Before storing uncooked whole chicken, discard the tight plastic wrappings and pour off any juices. Remove the neck and giblets from whole birds (sometimes these are in a plastic bag inside the cavity). Giblets should be cooked immediately or stored separately. Use the neck and giblets for stock; chop the liver to flavour a sauce, gravy or stuffing.

Loosely wrap the chicken in plastic wrap or place in a plastic bag, place the package on a plate and refrigerate on the bottom shelf of the refrigerator. Never place uncooked chicken where the juices could drip on or otherwise come into contact with other foodstuffs. A fresh, cleaned and wrapped chicken can be stored in the refrigerator for up to two days.

Storing cooked chicken: Chicken should stand no more than an hour at room temperature after cooking. If keeping longer than this, store it loosely wrapped in the refrigerator and use within three days. The chicken does not have to be cold when it goes into the refrigerator. If the chicken has a sauce or stuffing, it should be eaten within 24 hours of cooking. Stuffing and gravy should be stored separately.

The three basic chicken sizes, from left to right: large boiling fowl; roasting chicken; baby chicken or poussin.

Frozen chicken

Make sure that any frozen chicken you buy from the supermarket freezer is solid and completely enclosed in its packaging. Do not purchase any that appear semi-soft and that are sitting in their own juices, as this indicates that they have been in the display cabinet for longer than is ideal.

Freezing fresh chicken: Have the freezer temperature at minus 15°C or lower. Use suitable freezer bags and expel as much air as possible from the packaging; oxygen left behind will speed up the process of oxidisation, resulting in an unpleasant taste after prolonged storing. Uncooked, home-frozen chicken (without giblets) will keep for up to nine months in good condition. Remove the giblets before freezing as they will begin to deteriorate after eight weeks. If a package has partly defrosted it must never be refrozen; defrost fully in the refrigerator and cook promptly. Stuffed birds should never be frozen, as the filling will not freeze enough to prevent the development of harmful bacteria.

Freezing cooked chicken: Cooked whole chickens or chicken pieces can be frozen with or without bones, for up to two weeks. After this time it tends to dry out.

Moist chicken dishes such as stews, casseroles, curries and soups are all suitable for freezing.

Quickly reduce the temperature of the cooked item by placing it in the refrigerator to cool completely. Spoon the meat directly into plastic containers and seal, label and freeze. As a general rule, freeze cooked chicken for a maximum of two months.

Defrosting: Frozen chicken must be completely thawed in the refrigerator before cooking; allow two to three hours per 500 g (1 lb 2 oz). A frozen chicken should be cooked within 12 hours of thawing. Do not thaw chicken at room temperature.

Microwave defrosting is not recommended for whole frozen chickens because of uneven thawing. However, smaller packages of cuts or pre-cooked meals can be successfully thawed in the microwave using the defrost setting.

Always remove chicken from wrapping before defrosting. Stir casseroles occasionally to distribute heat evenly. Separate joints or pieces as they soften.

Preparation: Before cooking a chicken, remove the neck, giblets and fat pockets from the cavity. Discard the fat and use the neck and giblets for stock. Remove any excess fat and sinew from chicken pieces.

Raw poultry should be wiped with a damp cloth, rather than washed, before cooking.

Wipe frozen chickens with paper towels to absorb excess moisture.

Use a cook's knife for jointing uncooked chickens. Poultry shears are excellent for dividing whole chickens into serving portions, expecially for splitting the breastbone, cutting the backbone and rib bones and cutting the breast and legs in half.

Stuffing a whole chicken before roasting adds extra flavour and plumps up the chicken. Do not stuff a chicken more than three hours prior to cooking. If using warm stuffing, the chicken must be cooked immediately. Stuffed, or stuffed and trussed chickens take a little longer to cook than unstuffed chickens. The juices from the cavity of the chicken will soak into the stuffing, so the stuffing must be cooked through to prevent contamination with harmful salmonella bacteria.

Some people prefer chicken without the skin. Removing the skin eliminates much of the fat from the chicken, as the fat lies in a layer underneath the skin. Usually the skin is removed after cooking, but drumsticks can be skinned and then cooked. To remove the skin from drumsticks, use a small sharp knife. Begin by carefully loosening the skin from the flesh at the large joint end. Then pull the skin down and away from the flesh.

Chicken leg cuts, clockwise from left: thigh (underside view), drumstick, leg quarter (maryland), thigh fillet, thigh.

Chicken breast and wing cuts, clockwise from left: wing, single breast fillet, whole breast bone, tenderloin.

Carving

Let the cooked bird stand for 10 minutes in a warm place, covered loosely with foil. (This rests the meat and makes it easier to carve.) Place on a carving board or secure surface. Using a two-pronged fork to hold the bird and a sharp carving knife, cut around the leg, taking in a reasonable amount of flesh from the sides, firstly cutting through the skin and then using the tip of the knife to separate the bone at the joint. Cut above the wing joint, through the breastbone. Separate the legs by cutting into the thigh and drumstick.

Carve breast meat in slices parallel to the rib cage. Place pieces on a warmed serving platter with vegetables or directly onto serving plates.

Cut the chicken above the wing joint, through the breastbone.

Cut around the leg, cutting through the skin and then using the tip of the knife to separate the bone.

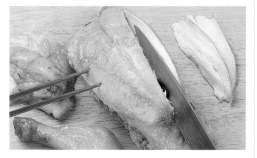
Carve the breast meat in even slices, parallel to the rib cage.

Jointing

Jointing a whole chicken is an easy process, once you know how. Large birds can be cut into four, six, eight or 10 pieces. Use a sharp, heavy knife or poultry shears.

To cut a bird into six pieces, remove the leg by cutting around the end of the thigh joint. Twist the leg sharply outwards to break the joint, and then cut through the joint. Turn the bird around and repeat on the other side. Remove the wings by bending them outwards and snipping around the joint.

Cut up one side of the body and open it out flat. Cut the body into two pieces. Cut down the centre of the breast to separate the two halves.

To make eight portions, separate the thigh from the drumstick. To make 10 portions, cut the breast pieces in half across the backbone.

Always keep in mind that the dark meat of a chicken (legs and thighs) takes longer to cook than the white meat of a chicken (breasts).

Twist the leg sharply outwards to break the joint, and then cut through the joint.

Remove the wings by bending them outwards and snipping around the joint.

Carefully cut up one side of the body and open it out flat.

Boning a whole chicken

Using a small, sharp knife, cut through the skin on the centre back. Separate the flesh from the bone down one side to the breast, being careful not to pierce the skin.

Follow along the bones closely with the knife, gradually easing the meat from the thigh, drumstick and wing. Cut through the thigh bone and cut off the wing tip. Repeat on the other side, then lift the ribcage away, leaving the flesh in one piece. Scrape all the meat from the drumstick and wings; discard the bones.

Turn the wing and drumstick flesh inside the chicken and lay the chicken out flat, skin side down. The chicken is now ready to be stuffed and rolled according to a recipe.

Using a small sharp knife, cut through the chicken skin and along the backbone.

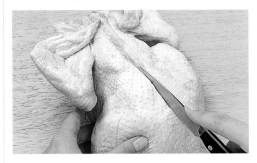

Using the tip of the knife, scrape against the bone down the length of the cut.

Cut through the thigh bone and cut off the wing tip, then lift out the rib cage.

Scrape all of the flesh from the drumsticks and wings and discard the leg bones.

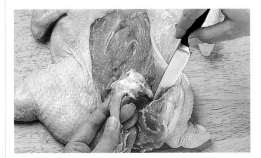

Remove the wing bones and turn the flesh inside the chicken.

Turn the wing and drumstick flesh inside the chicken and lay the chicken out flat.

Stuffing

Spoon the stuffing mixture loosely into the cavity of the chicken. Secure the skin across the cavity with a skewer. Trussing a whole chicken keeps the stuffing in place and holds the chicken together. Fill the chicken with the stuffing and pull the skin down over the cavity. Turn the chicken over onto its breast and tie a long length of kitchen string around the wings, securing them neatly. Turn the chicken over, taking the string over the legs and crossing it underneath and tie the legs together firmly. Remove all the strings before carving.

Spoon the stuffing mixture into the tail cavity, allowing for expansion during cooking.

Secure the skin across the cavity with a skewer.

Tuck the tail (the parson's nose) into the cavity and tie the legs together.

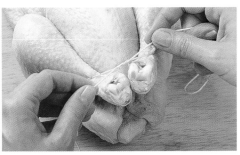

Index

Index

Published in 2009 by Murdoch Books Pty Limited.

Murdoch Books Australia
Pier 8/9, 23 Hickson Road
Millers Point NSW 2000
Phone: + 61 (0) 2 8220 2000
Fax: + 61 (0) 2 8220 2558
www.murdochbooks.com.au

Murdoch Books UK Limited
Erico House, 6th Floor
93–99 Upper Richmond Road
Putney, London SW15 2TG
Phone: +44 (0) 20 8785 5995
Fax: +44 (0) 20 8785 5985
www.murdochbooks.co.uk

Chief Executive: Juliet Rogers
Publishing Director: Kay Scarlett

Project manager and editor: Kristin Buesing
Design concept: Heather Menzies
Design: Heather Menzies and Jacqueline Richards
Photographer: Natasha Milne
Stylist: Kate Brown
Food preparation: Peta Dent, Kirrily La Rosa, Wendy Quisumbing
Introduction text: Leanne Kitchen
Production: Kita George

National Library of Australia Cataloguing-in-Publication Data
Homestyle chicken. Includes index.
ISBN 9781741961669 (pbk.)
Cookery (chicken). 641.665

A catalogue record for this book is available from the British Library.
Colour separation by Splitting Image in Clayton, Victoria, Australia.
Printed by i-Book Printing Ltd. in 2009. PRINTED IN CHINA.

IMPORTANT: Those who might be at risk from the effects of salmonella poisoning
(the elderly, pregnant women, young children and those suffering from immune deficiency diseases)
should consult their doctor with any concerns about eating raw eggs.

CONVERSION GUIDE: You may find cooking times vary depending on the oven
you are using. For fan-forced ovens, as a general rule, set the oven temperature
to 20°C (35°F) lower than indicated in the recipe.